P9-DVP-980

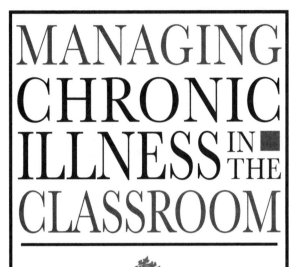

# MANAGING CHRONIC ILLNESS IN THE CLASSROOM

by Dorothy Botsch Wishnietsky
and Dan H. Wishnietsky

LCCC LIBRARY

DISCARD

Published by
Phi Delta Kappa Educational Foundation
Bloomington, Indiana

Cover design by Victoria Voelker

LC
4545
.W57
1996
PAP

Library of Congress Catalog Card Number 96-67187
ISBN 0-87367-487-1
Copyright © 1996 by Dorothy Botsch Wishnietsky
and Dan H. Wishnietsky
Bloomington, Indiana

To our parents:

Emil and Margaret Botsch

Ben and Naomi Wishnietsky

# Table of Contents

# Introduction

An important but often overlooked member of a student's health care team is the teacher. Children and adolescents spend an average of 35 hours each week at school. Students with chronic illnesses can present special challenges for which the teacher must be prepared. For example, a student with epilepsy may have a seizure in the classroom, a student with sickle cell disease may have a painful episode, or a student with arthritis may need classroom adaptations or physical therapy during the school day. Each of these circumstances requires a different mode of management. And events that have the same medical identification, such as a "seizure," can vary dramatically in appearance and type of response or care that will be required.

Teachers who understand the chronic illnesses of their students will feel more comfortable, be better able to handle illness-related situations calmly and effectively, and may even help prevent further medical problems. For example, when a teacher has a student with insulin-dependent diabetes, the most common problem that will require the teacher's attention is low blood sugar. Teachers who are familiar with the signs of low blood sugar can provide an appropriate intervention, such as giving the student four ounces of juice, before the student becomes disoriented or perhaps loses consciousness. Informed teachers also can observe and report changes in their students' physical appearance or behavior that will help parents or guardians work more effectively with physicians and other health care providers.

Academic performance can be affected by such factors as medication, absenteeism, physical effects of illness, and prescribed therapy. By providing appropriate interventions, the classroom teacher can develop an environment in which the student can perform at his or her full potential and participate fully in school activities.

The disease is not the student. Although a student has a chronic illness, he or she has the same educational needs as other students.

This also is true for social needs. The informed teacher can help solve psychosocial problems that arise because of chronic illness. In many cases, students with chronic illnesses experience increased physical and emotional stress that may adversely affect self-esteem and feelings of self-worth. Teachers, along with parents and health care providers, can evaluate the student's needs and develop a classroom environment in which chronically ill students feel accepted and valued.

We have designed this book to inform educators about the special needs of students with a chronic illness, how to recognize health events that may interfere with learning, and how to intervene when appropriate. Chapter One offers a general overview in which we discuss the social, psychological, and physical needs of students with a chronic illness. In this chapter we also delineate the responsibilities of teachers, administrators, and parents or guardians.

Chapters Two through Nine include information about eight chronic illnesses frequently encountered by teachers: AIDS, arthritis, asthma, cancer, cystic fibrosis, diabetes, epilepsy, and sickle cell disease. Each chapter explains the disease, its treatment and effects, management procedures, and how to recognize when teacher intervention is required. Chapter Ten provides sources of additional information about chronic illness and suggestions about how educators can better prepare themselves for meeting the needs of students who have these illnesses. Finally, we include a resource list of sources for additional information about the chronic illnesses addressed in this volume and other chronic illnesses affecting the young, such as multiple sclerosis.

The information in this volume is general. We present it to alert educators to problems that can affect students' physical and emotional health and school performance. This book is not intended to be a medical text. Nor should teachers attempt to use the interventions described in this book without consulting with the student's parents, school authorities, or medical authorities. Additional facts about each of the chronic illnesses described in Chapters Two through Nine may be obtained by contacting medical professionals or the professional associations listed in the Resources section. The information in this book is a starting point for teachers and other caregivers to become informed about chronic illnesses and their effects on students who may be in their classrooms. Such information will assist teachers in better serving chronically ill students.

In closing, we wish to thank Barbara A. Hackman, R.N., M.S., C.S., P.N.P., Clinical Nurse Specialist in Pediatrics at the North Carolina Baptist Hospital in Winston-Salem, for reviewing the manuscript and for her many helpful suggestions.

# Chapter One

# The Classroom Environment

Most teachers will face the challenges of teaching one or more students who have a chronic illness. Information from the Department of Health and Human Services indicates that approximately 1%, or more than one million, of the children in the United States have a severe chronic illness. These are students whose lives are limited by severe asthma, arthritis, cancer, diabetes, cystic fibrosis, epilepsy, HIV/AIDS, sickle cell disease, or other conditions. Published data from medical associations and foundations, such as the American Diabetes Association or the Epilepsy Foundation of America, indicate that almost one child in 600 develops insulin-dependent diabetes; about 300,000 children have seizure disorders; more than 100,000 infants, adolescents, and teenagers have arthritis; and about one in 375 African-American children has sickle cell disease. According to the 1992 National Health Interview Survey, when chronic illness is defined as a condition that is expected to last more than three months and limits school performance, about 5% of all students qualify as chronically ill.

## Defining a Chronic Illness

Educators are familiar with common, *acute* illnesses, such as the common cold and influenza. Such common illnesses occur each year and often cause students to miss a few days of school. And then the student gets well. An acute illness develops quickly, lasts for a limited time, sometimes can be prevented, and can be cured. Acute illnesses usually are caused by bacteria or a virus, and research has discovered much about such diseases. Less than a century ago many acute illnesses could be fatal, such as tuberculosis and pneumonia and such childhood diseases as measles, mumps, and chicken pox. Because of research and better medicines, today these illnesses not only are curable but most can be prevented.

A *chronic* illness is different from an acute illness. It may develop slowly, go undetected for years, and often will last a lifetime. Instead of being caused by an external agent, such as bacteria or a virus, the cause may be internal, such as the immune system opposing itself or an internal organ failing to function. Chronic illnesses are seldom cured, but often they can be controlled using diet, exercise, and medication and by improving the quality of personal relationships.

Even when students maintain a daily routine to control the disease, the expected outcomes may not be achieved. The course of many chronic illnesses cannot be predicted with certainty. In many cases the symptoms can occur at any time. Most students with chronic illnesses maintain routines that include tests, medication, therapy, and periodic medical visits. Although the hope for a cure often is present, the reality for many chronically ill students is that they must maintain a style of living that is limited to a greater or lesser extent when compared to that of healthy students.

The effects of a chronic illness vary over time and according to the nature of the illness. Some chronically ill students will experience periods of improvement or remission because of treatment or some other reason. Students with cancer provide an example. The goal of cancer treatment is to remove or destroy abnormal (cancerous) cells. When remission occurs, everyone involved hopes that the cancer has been eradicated. However, if a recurrence or relapse occurs, treatment must begin anew. Thus the student who has cancer may have periods of relatively good health alternating with periods of severe limitation resulting from the disease itself or its treatment.

Other illnesses present other patterns. In insulin-dependent diabetes, for example, the pancreas produces little or no insulin. Sometimes, shortly after diagnosis, the pancreas briefly recuperates and external insulin needs decrease. However, this "honeymoon period" usually is short-lived, and the regimen associated with insulin-dependent diabetes must be resumed.

## The Student Is Not the Disease

Having a chronic illness greatly influences the affected student's relationships, emotions, self-esteem, feelings of security, and independence. Acute illnesses may produce similar effects; but the physical, lifestyle, and emotional changes that take place during an acute illness usually are temporary. Changes caused by chronic illnesses typically are permanent.

Indeed, society's attitudes toward chronic illnesses convey a sense of permanence. A person with diabetes is called a diabetic, a person with arthritis is arthritic, and a person with asthma is labeled asthmatic. The person *becomes* the disease.

Teachers can help to limit the negative social and emotional effects of a chronic illness by recognizing that the student is not the disease. After all, the student who has an acute illness such as the flu is not called a "fluic." The student simply is a person with the flu. In a similar spirit, a student with a chronic illness such as diabetes should not be referred to as a diabetic, but rather as a student with diabetes. This simple distinction will help chronically ill students discover their identity not in the illness but in who they are. A chronic illness cannot and should not be ignored; it is a part of the student's life. But the illness is not the most important part of that life.

Like their peers, students with a chronic illness require love, support, understanding, and the full benefits of education. Classroom or general school modifications may be necessary because of physical limitations, but these accommodations should not receive undue attention. An example of such a modification might be simply arranging for a friend of a student with arthritis to carry

7

the affected student's books or providing a second set of textbooks for the student's home so that the student does not have to carry books back and forth. Another example is adjusting assignment deadlines for students with cancer to accommodate their treatment schedule.

Teachers should guard against becoming overprotective. Students with a chronic illness should be evaluated in terms of academics and discipline using the same standards applied to the rest of the class. Doing so helps to instill in the affected student a pride in learning and also helps to establish camaraderie among all students. Adolescent students, in particular, want to feel as though they are part of the class and not different or abnormal because of the effects of a chronic illness on their body or lifestyle. Even when a student's medical condition precludes full-time attendance, teachers should include that student in as many activities as possible. Depending on the situation, assignments can be sent home or to the hospital, the school can provide a tutor, or the student can attend school part of the day.

All students experience physical, psychological, and social pressures, but having a chronic illness produces additional anxiety and apprehension. Such factors as recurrent pain, hospitalization, therapeutic procedures, school absences, and illness-related financial pressures may produce feelings of worry, inferiority, hopelessness, or guilt. Many students adapt well to the stresses of a chronic illness; others do not. Teachers should be alert to learning or behavioral changes that may result from such stresses and report them to the professionals involved in the student's health care. By communicating with parents and health care professionals, teachers will be better able to develop appropriate interventions that can minimize the student's frustrations with school and increase the student's confidence and self-esteem.

## Age Makes a Difference

As students mature, they react differently to such concerns as peer acceptance, body image, self-worth, and independence. Maturation also affects the way students react to their chronic illness. For example, young children with diabetes may not be able to indicate when they are experiencing low blood sugar. Thus for younger students, it is imperative that the classroom teacher be familiar with the signs of low blood sugar and intervene appropriately. Young students also are just beginning to exert their independence and may attempt to exert control by purposely exhibiting unhealthy behaviors. If this occurs, experts suggest giving the student a greater measure of control over the situation and using positive reinforcement.

As chronically ill students grow older, feelings of insecurity may develop because they see themselves as being different from their peers. These insecurities also increase their need for independence. Thus teachers should allow students with chronic illness to be independent whenever possible and not call attention to the tasks associated with the illness. For example, a student with sickle cell disease (which often damages kidney tissues) may need to use the toilet frequently and may need to drink large amounts of fluid to prevent dehydration. The teacher should permit the student to leave the classroom to use the restroom or drinking fountain without interrupting the class to ask permission. When classmates notice that a student with a chronic illness is accommodated in some way, they should be encouraged to ask questions. Likewise, chronically ill students should be encouraged and allowed to share their knowledge and feelings about their medical condition. But the amount of information shared with classmates should be the decision of the affected student, not the teacher.

A concern of many medical professionals is that when students exert their independence, they may spend less time controlling their chronic illness. Teenagers often think of themselves as indestructible and ignore their health. A student with diabetes may skip an insulin injection, or a student with arthritis may resist the physical therapy designed to prevent or minimize his or her disabilities. Older students also may rebel if parents or teachers criticize their unhealthy behaviors or demand changes. As with younger students, the best response that teachers and parents can make is to be positive and understanding, allowing the student to have reasonable control of the situation.

## Parent Expectations

A chronic illness affects the entire family. When a child is diagnosed with a chronic illness, all members of the family experience emotional upheaval. Many psychologists suggest that the emotional stages that family members feel are the same as when a family member dies. These include denial, anger and depression, bargaining, and finally acceptance. With acceptance, the family usually takes two positive steps: 1) They become experts on the medical condition, and 2) they do all that is possible to control the physical and emotional aspects of the illness. Part of controlling the effects of the disease is working with the school staff.

Before the beginning of the school year or when the child changes schools, the parent or guardian should schedule a conference with the student's teachers, principal, and school nurse. If the student's record indicates a chronic illness and the parent does not schedule such a conference, then school personnel should initiate the dialogue. This meeting will provide the educators with key information concerning the chronic illness and will establish a forum for addressing the student's needs. Topics that should be addressed include the child's education and care plan while at school, who will be the primary contact between the parent and the school, and what steps should be taken in case of a medical emergency.

An effective education and care plan is a written document that clearly states how the student's health care needs will be met while at school so that he or she will have the most appropriate and least restrictive education. The plan should include curriculum, medications, medical testing, limits on activities, locations of classes, meals, meal schedules, emergency contacts, and other parent and teacher concerns. Part of the plan also should be a self-care component that states the student's responsibility for managing his or her medical condition. In addition to presenting the education and care plan in written form, the plan's specifications should be discussed in a parent-educator conference with the student present. In that way everyone involved will know what to expect, and the student will be able to recognize whether the plan is being followed. Such a plan should cover the full academic year, but it may be modified during the year as needed.

Parents and guardians rightly expect cooperation from the school faculty and staff. They expect that all educators involved with their child will be informed regarding the education and care plan and will follow its requirements. If an emergency occurs, the parent expects to be contacted promptly. It is the parents' responsibility to provide the school with any required written requests for medical care; in almost all cases, school personnel cannot legally act on verbal requests. For example, when a student with a chronic illness needs to take medication at school, written instructions describing the treatment from the student's physician must be on file at the school. Teachers also should expect the parents of students with a chronic illness to closely monitor their child's progress and to communicate often with the school. The Individuals with Disabilities Education Act of 1990 established parents' right to question placement decisions and their right to due process when differences of opinion arise. (See Phi Delta Kappa fastback 360 *Implementing the Disabilities Acts: Implications for Educators* by Patricia F. First and Joan L. Curcio.)

## Legal Responsibilities

Although schools and districts may vary in the level of available health care assistance, federal law requires that every public school provide adequate services for students with chronic illnesses. Under federal law, chronic illnesses usually are considered a disability; and people with such illnesses are legally protected from discrimination. Federal laws require public schools to provide disabled students with a free, appropriate education in the least restrictive environment. Special services, based on the type of illness and its effects, also are ensured. These services may include transportation, audiology, recreation, school health services, psychological services, physical and occupational therapy, speech and language therapy, assistive technology, and social work services.

When a school's administration is advised that a student has a chronic illness, personnel must evaluate the student's special needs and develop a plan for satisfying any medical requirements. The plan, known as an individual education plan (IEP), is developed by school personnel working with parents, medical specialists, psychologists, and sociologists. Each student's needs are assessed, and the individual education plan defines how the school will deliver the services and assistance the student requires in order to have equitable access all school programs. The plan must be updated, approved, and signed by the parent or guardian each academic year. Once the IEP is in place, it cannot be altered without parent consent. In addition, a member of the school faculty or staff is assigned to implement the plan and to inform other school personnel of their responsibilities under the plan.

Some students with certain chronic illnesses are eligible for vocational education. An example is a student with arthritis whose disease requires occupational and physical therapy. This plan, called an individual vocational education plan, is similar to the individual education plan except that the plan focuses on vocational education rather than all school programs.

The law prohibits all schools that receive federal funds from discriminating against students with a chronic illness. Parents of chronically ill students may rightfully expect these plans to be developed and enacted. If they believe that their child's rights are not being protected or their child's needs are not being met, they may appeal to the courts.

## Healthful Learning Environments

One distinction of a healthful learning environment is that all students, including students with chronic illnesses, are fully involved in school activities. Implementing this type of setting requires a variety of services, allowances, and modifications, because each student is different and chronic illnesses manifest themselves in various ways. The chronic illness might be "hidden" with few, if any, outward signs. Or the disease might require daily injections or confine the student to a wheelchair. Extensive differences also occur among students with the same chronic illness. A student with childhood arthritis may have swollen joints that are not noticeable except for a visible stiffness when performing certain tasks. Another student with childhood arthritis might not be able to move without pain or might require crutches or a wheelchair. In the first case an appropriate accommodation for the student might be simply to allow extra time to complete an assignment. The second student probably would require a number of special services, accommodations, and classroom modifications to succeed in school.

An outline for developing each student's healthful learning environment will be written in the student's individual education plan or individual vocational education plan. As that plan is developed, a major consideration will be to provide an environment in which the student can manage his or her condition easily and without embarrassment. Doing so can be challenging. For example, one incident that required intervention concerned a student with diabetes. Workers in the cafeteria knew about the diabetes and so they tried to be helpful by checking the tray each day to be certain that the student was eating a healthy meal. However, this checking so embarrassed the youngster that the student stopped eating lunch and started having low blood sugar in the afternoon. When the mother realized the problem, she met with the school staff and asked the cafeteria workers not to check the student's food choices so that her child could eat without being embarrassed. This solved both the social and the medical problems.

School personnel need to support student self-care without being overly protective. Examples include allowing students to administer their own medication and to perform required tests or exercises. However, because of legal concerns, strict procedures may be required when medications are involved. Medical needs should be specified in the IEP and understood by the student, his or her parents, teachers, and other school personnel. However, regardless of the circumstances, medication should be viewed as routine, not a special occurrence. Such problems as students forgetting to take medication usually can be solved using subtle supervision and encouragement. Also, when students with chronic illnesses do not follow their required medical regimen, they should not be considered a discipline problem. Such difficulties should be referred to the parents or medical personnel when they cannot be resolved by school staff.

An atmosphere of acceptance and support also is required when students with chronic illnesses perform required tests or exercises while in class. For example, a student with cystic fibrosis often has to cough to help dislodge mucus from his or her airways. Sometimes the student feels embarrassed to cough in class. Since people with cystic fibrosis should never try to restrain coughing, teachers should promote an academic environment in which the student is comfortable performing medically appropriate behaviors. Students with cystic fibrosis should have tissues readily available and should be able to leave class easily for medical reasons. Teachers should help other students realize that such coughing is appropriate and not a cause for comment or distraction.

A healthy learning environment also provides chronically ill students with required special services. These services can range from minor adaptations, such as having most classes on the same floor of the school, to major academic services, such as home schooling. To determine what special services are necessary, school personnel, parents, and medical personnel meet to evaluate the student's needs. After the special services are identified, they are recorded and become part of the student's IEP. The IEP conference report explains and describes the services that the student will receive, the goals of such services, how the school personnel will measure attainment of those goals, and how the services will be delivered. Of the services available through school systems, some of the major types include tutoring, special education, counseling, health monitoring, adaptive learning, evaluative testing, and transportation.

## Education About Chronic Illnesses

Study of major chronic illnesses and their treatment and effects should be included in health and science curricula. Such study should be an integral part of these curricula at all levels, not an add-on. To supplement student and teacher discussions, personnel from local medical centers or professional societies, such as the Epilepsy Foundation of America or the Cystic Fibrosis Foundation, might be invited to make presentations to classes.

If a student with the chronic illness under discussion is a member of the class, we recommend that the student and his or her parents be advised of the lesson and the student be given the option of not attending the class during that lesson. The chronically ill student may feel uncomfortable being the center of the class discussion and so should have the option of avoiding embarrassment. However, many students with chronic illnesses will prefer to answer questions and to discuss their illness with their classmates. Some students with chronic illnesses are even willing to demonstrate some of the medical procedures they use to keep their illness in control. For example, students with diabetes can talk about how they monitor their blood sugar and demonstrate how blood sugar is measured using a blood-glucose meter. In all cases, the chronically ill students should be in control when they are answering questions or making a demonstration. Educators should not pressure these students to discuss things about their diseases that make them feel uncomfortable.

A standard procedure in education, whether preservice or inservice training, is to instruct teachers and administrators about the potential educational, social, and psychological needs of their students and how to address those needs. Students with chronic illnesses have long-term medical needs that affect their education and that also need to be addressed by educators. This book is intended to be a starting point. The chapters that follow present basic information about seven prevalent chronic illnesses: arthritis, asthma, cancer, diabetes, cystic fibrosis, epilepsy, and sickle cell disease. In addition, we include a chapter on an illness that, unfortunately, is becoming more common in schools: AIDS and HIV infection. Our goal in writing these chapters is not to redefine the teacher or the administrator as a medical professional, but rather to enhance the reader's knowledge of chronic illnesses, the needs of chronically ill students, and how best to meet those needs.

# Chapter Two

# AIDS and HIV Infection

AIDS (acquired immunodeficiency syndrome) has become an ominous aspect of American life. Experts estimate that between 10,000 and 20,000 children in the United States are infected with HIV (human immunodeficiency virus), the virus that leads to AIDS, or have AIDS.

Approximately 7,000 infants are born each year to HIV-infected women, and about 25% of these children become infected with the virus. When children are born with HIV, about 14% develop AIDS and die in the first year. The average life expectancy past the first year for a child born with HIV is 8½ years. Approximately 75% of children with HIV are either African American or Latino, with the majority being African American. In 1991, AIDS was the seventh leading cause of death in children ages 1 to 4 years.

The Centers for Disease Control and Prevention (commonly referred to as the CDC) report that AIDS is the sixth leading cause of death in adolescents and young adults ages 15 through 24. The fastest growing population of young people with HIV are female and were infected with HIV through heterosexual contact. Here again, 72% are either African American or Latino.

HIV infection knows no boundaries and is growing just as fast in rural America as it is in the larger urban areas. It has become not only a health issue but also a social and moral issue because sexual contact and illegal drug use are the most common modes of transmission.

Absent a cure, the best weapons to fight the HIV virus are education and prevention. Therefore, educators need to be well-informed about HIV and AIDS. Parents and members of the community beyond the schools also must become involved in order to make HIV/AIDS education comprehensive and thorough and to provide the appropriate supports to promote HIV prevention and to care for those affected by HIV and AIDS.

## What Are AIDS and HIV?

AIDS is the eventual failure of the body's immune system caused by the human immunodeficiency virus. A "syndrome" rather than a single disease, AIDS causes the body to be unable to ward off potentially fatal diseases, and so the affected individual eventually dies from one or several AIDS-related illnesses. AIDS first was recognized and described in 1984, although the earliest documented cases appeared in 1980. Many researchers now believe that AIDS existed decades before these earliest cases were described. However, the origin of AIDS is not known.

Since the late 1980s, researchers have learned much about HIV and have developed several drugs that slow the development of AIDS after infection. Transmission of HIV is through contact with blood and body fluids, such as semen, vaginal fluid, or breast milk. It is not passed through casual contacts, such as being near an HIV-infected person who is coughing or sneezing, kissing an infected individual, wiping his or her tears, or touching, hugging, or sharing bathrooms, food, or eating utensils with an infected person. Other body fluids, such as vomit, saliva, urine, and feces do not carry HIV. (However, these fluids may carry other diseases such as, colds, flu, Hepatitis A, and cytomegalovirus [CMV].)

HIV is different from other viruses in that it is a chronic infection associated with the progressive deterioration of the body's immune system. Every day the body is invaded by a multitude of viruses, bacteria, parasites, fungi, and foreign particles that come from the environment, such as through the air when another person coughs or sneezes. Humans have a built-in defense system, called the immune system, to fight off these invaders. The immune system is composed of the white blood cells, or lymphocytes. The lymphocytes, T cells and B cells, help to fight off these invaders so that the body stays healthy most of the time.

When people are affected by a virus or other infection, in most cases the illness lasts for only a short time because the T cells and B cells eventually overcome the invader, and the person returns to good health. However, when HIV infects the body, the virus kills T cells. As more T cells die, the body loses its ability to fight viruses, bacteria, and so on. Thus the person with HIV is prone to develop infections that otherwise would not occur. People with HIV are said to have AIDS when they have a very low T cell count and they have a serious illness or infection associated with HIV.

The body also protects itself from infections by producing antibodies. Antibodies are specialized proteins in the blood that recognize and fight foreign substances and provide immunity from their harmful effects. Once antibodies are produced, they remain in the blood indefinitely. Thus, once a person experiences a specific virus, he or she should not be affected again because of the immunity produced by the antibodies. For example, when a youngster has chicken pox, he or she is then immune to that disease for life.

The body also develops antibodies to fight and destroy HIV. However, these antibodies are not fully effective and become less effective over time. One way to detect HIV in a person is to screen for these specific antibodies. When a person has the HIV antibodies, that person is described as "HIV positive."

The time between acquiring the virus and the body's production of the antibodies may be several months. Six months is commonly cited. Therefore, if an individual has engaged in risky behavior, he or she may not test positive for some time.

Information about HIV transmission and prevention has been disseminated widely. Although AIDS in the United States initially was associated with homosexual behavior and illegal drug use that involves sharing needles, HIV infection has grown to epidemic proportions across all segments of the population. Unprotected sexual activity and drug abuse still are the primary modes of transmission of the virus.

During the teenage years, in particular, when sexual exploration and experimentation with drugs is most widespread, particular attention needs to be paid to helping students understand the risks associated with their behaviors. Studies indicate that the average age at which an individual first experiences sexual intercourse is 16. More than half of the students in grades 9 through 12 who participated in a CDC survey reported having sexual intercourse at least once, and only 46% of them used a condom in their most recent experience. Of the students with four or more partners, only 41% of them used condoms.

These are frightening statistics, because an individual may go for years without knowing that he or she carries HIV. Thus the individual may unknowingly infect others during the incubation time for HIV, which can range from a few months to 10 years. Many of today's young adults with AIDS acquired HIV when they were teenagers in middle or high school.

## HIV Infection in Children

Children who are born with HIV acquired the infection from their mothers during the pregnancy through shared maternal blood, during the birth process, or from breast milk after birth. Prior to 1985, some infants and children became infected with HIV through blood transfusions or from a blood clotting factor given to children with hemophilia (an inherited bleeding disorder). Today, the risk of acquiring HIV through blood products has decreased to 1 in 225,000 transfusions because of better blood-screening methods. Children who have been sexually abused by an infected person are at risk for HIV.

There are several stages of the HIV infection, and children go through them at different rates. Infants who are at high risk for developing HIV from their mother should be tested at 1 month of age, again at 4 months of age and, if still negative, at 18 months of age. The reason for this is, first, maternal blood is still in the infant at birth, and the infant probably would test positive for HIV antibodies. After about 1 month, the maternal antibodies are gone; and the infant will begin to develop his or her own antibodies to HIV if it is present. The periodic testing will help to give a more decisive negative if the child does not have HIV. During this testing time, the child is said to have indeterminate infection.

If the HIV antibody test is positive and the child shows no symptoms, this stage is labeled asymptomatic infection. Once symptoms are present, the condition is labeled symptomatic infection. The progression to serious and specific infections and symptoms determines the diagnosis of AIDS. Early symptoms of HIV in children include a broad spectrum of opportunistic infections and problems that are not AIDS defining. These include oral thrush, recurrent fevers, failure to grow and gain weight normally, and increased severity of usual childhood problems, such as ear infections and sinus infections. It is very important for children with HIV to be thoroughly immunized and to see their physician regularly in order to prevent many childhood diseases that could be serious for them. In some cases, children with HIV also may be developmentally delayed and may be short in stature.

The later stages of HIV, which define the AIDS diagnosis, involve serious opportunistic infections, such as LIP (lymphoid interstitial pneumonitis), severe bacterial infections, PCP (pneumocystis carinii pneumonia, or wasting syndrome), encephalopathy (which causes neurological deficits), and certain cancers. Childhood AIDS differs from adult AIDS in that it is very rare for a child to develop Kaposi's sarcoma, which is a serious cancer in adults with AIDS. Also, young children with HIV generally become ill more rapidly than adults and adolescents with HIV, especially infants who develop AIDS symptoms during the first year of life.

## Managing HIV and AIDS

Survival rates for children and adolescents vary greatly but have improved with advances in medical management of HIV and opportunistic infections. Although there is no medically documented case of a cure, many people are surviving for long periods with HIV. For this reason, HIV infection now is labeled as life-threatening rather than fatal.

There are five basic components to the management of HIV:

1. Identification of HIV infection through antibody testing.

2. Antiretroviral treatment, which involves placing the child on a drug that blocks the reproduction of the virus. The most common drugs used are zidovudine (called AZT), didanosine (ddI), and zalcitabine (ddC). Often a combination of these drugs is used.

3. Prophylaxis, or preventive medication. For example, some medicines are used to prevent pneumonias and other infections that may occur. Some of the drugs used are the sulfa drugs, Bactrim or Septra, Dapsone, and pentamidine. Children also may benefit from intravenous infusions of immunoglobulin about once a month, which helps their immune system fight bacterial infections.

4. Treatment of active infections. For the student with an HIV-weakened immune system, many types of infection can be life-threatening. Precautions for the HIV-positive student are similar to those for the student with cancer whose immune system is suppressed by chemotherapy (see Chapter 5). Of special concern are the few infections for which there is no safe and effective treatment.

5. Supportive care. Management of HIV involves professionals from many disciplines, including physicians and nurses of many specialties, social workers, nutritionists, pharmacists, developmental specialists, clergy, teachers, guidance counselors, physical therapists, language therapists, and speech therapists. These professionals should work closely with families in order to provide the quality of care that each family needs.

## How Schools Should Respond

Students with HIV come from all types of families. The majority of younger children infected with HIV acquired it during the mother's pregnancy, and so one or both parents also are infected. In some cases, infected children live with extended family members, with friends of the family, or in foster care or adoptive homes. Children of parents who acquired HIV through drug abuse also may have emotional and behavioral problems because of their perinatal environment and may need special supportive assistance at school.

Many families that are struggling with HIV and AIDS also struggle with poverty, poor access to health care, substandard living conditions, and related problems. A strong community effort is needed to provide these students and their families with supportive care, such as adequate housing, nutrition, transportation, legal services, and respite care. Hospice is an extremely useful service for families living with the final stages of AIDS.

Families living with HIV require access to care and services. Caretakers of children with HIV should be accepted as members of the health care team and full partners in making health care decisions. They need complete and accurate information regarding treatment choices and anything else involving the student. These families also need respect for their privacy and confidentiality. Care systems, in which the school is a vital part, need to be comprehensive, coordinated, community-based, family-centered, and culturally competent.

*The School's Legal Requirements Regarding HIV and AIDS.* Laws regarding reporting HIV-infected individuals vary from state to state. Currently only 26 states require HIV reporting. Therefore, many schools may not be notified that they have a student with HIV. Notification often is left up to the student's parents and physician. Many parents prefer that the HIV infection be kept confidential to prevent discrimination and emotional trauma for the child. In many states, the only time a physician can report

23

an HIV infection to the local school personnel is when the student poses a threat of transmission to others, for example, if the infected student has an open wound or exhibits a behavioral disorder that involves biting. After a formal evaluation, such a student may be placed in an alternate childcare or school setting that minimizes the risk of transmitting the virus to other students or teachers.

*Universal Precautions.* The standard for "universal precautions" is to assume that everyone is a potential carrier of HIV or other viruses or bacteria.

The key principal of the universal precautions is avoiding all contact with another person's blood or body fluids. Teachers and administrators should have access to latex gloves to wear when attending to scrapes, cuts, and nosebleeds at school. Playground supervisors and physical education instructors should carry a pair of latex gloves in their pocket in case of a mishap. When an individual does come in contact with another person's blood, he or she should immediately wash the contact area with soap and water. Blood spills should be cleaned using a mixture of 9 parts water to 1 part bleach.

Each school system should have a written blood and body fluid exposure policy. And a curriculum unit about HIV and AIDS should include teaching students not to come in contact with another person's blood. Students also should be instructed to report finding used syringes and needles around the school or in their neighborhood. They should be taught that it may be dangerous to pick up these items.

Fortunately, HIV is a very fragile virus outside of the human body. There has never been a confirmed case of anyone being infected with HIV at school. However, the potential for infection exists whenever a student gets a cut or a wound is exposed. It is vital for teachers, other school personnel, and students to be well-informed about HIV and to learn and use universal precautions. Almost every state has a toll-free AIDS hotline for obtaining information. The National AIDS Hotline in the United States can be reached by calling 1-800-342-AIDS.

## Talking with Students About HIV and AIDS

AIDS and HIV infection raise difficult issues that many adults are uncomfortable discussing. However, AIDS is a part of the environment and information (and misinformation) about AIDS can be found in every communications medium. Even very young children are beginning to ask questions about AIDS.

Often, younger students cannot distinguish between casual and non-casual transmission. They may mistakenly believe that they can catch AIDS as easily as they or their classmates have caught a cold or chicken pox. Therefore, it is important for teachers to assure students, first of all, that catching AIDS is not easy.

In progressive, age-appropriate steps, students should be taught more about HIV infection and AIDS. Such information should be integrated into health and science units in all grades. And teachers should be prepared to answer students' questions openly and honestly.

Adolescents during the middle and high school years, in particular, need to know that certain behaviors may place them at serious risk of HIV infection. Teachers need to be candid when answering students' questions about sexual experimentation and intercourse and about using intravenous drugs. And these issues merit specific inclusion in the curriculum, however uncomfortable the discussion makes educators, students, and parents. HIV and AIDS are matters of life and death.

# Chapter Three

# Juvenile Arthritis

Many people associate arthritis with the elderly. But in the United States, slightly fewer than 3 in every 1,000 young people have some form of this disease. *Arthritis* is a general term that refers to the more than 100 pathological conditions of the joints, tendons, muscles, bones, and nerves. Known as rheumatic diseases, these conditions often cause pain, swelling, redness, and loss of motion in the tissues surrounding the joints. Arthritis is not contagious.

Some forms of arthritis affect other parts of the body, such as the skin or internal organs. Arthritis also may hinder growth, causing a young person to be small for his or her age or to have a stiff walk that results in taking short steps. In some cases, the effects of arthritis are hidden and the affected youngster shows few, if any, outward signs of the disease. Even quite swollen joints may go unnoticed by teachers; and if the student does not complain of swelling or pain, then the teacher may not realize the limitations caused by the disease. This is especially true when students with arthritis, attempting to be like the other students, try to ignore or conceal their illness.

## Juvenile Rheumatoid Arthritis

The most common form of arthritis that affects young people is juvenile rheumatoid arthritis (JRA). The exact cause of JRA has not been identified. Scientists do know that arthritis involves irregularities of the immune system. The purpose of the immune system is to defend the body against harmful substances, such as bacteria or viruses. When a person has an autoimmune disease such as juvenile rheumatoid arthritis, some of the white blood cells of the immune system are unable to distinguish body tissue from foreign substances. This causes the immune system to release chemicals that are intended to destroy bacteria or viruses, but actually cause inflammation, a process that causes the body to damage itself.

Two examples of inflammation caused by JRA are: 1) painful swelling near a joint or 2) inflammation near the iris of the eye. Usually arthritis inflammations are mild and cause few problems. But severe cases may result in extreme pain and joint stiffness that makes movement difficult. Periods of pain may vary from day to day or from morning to afternoon. Times when the arthritis is especially painful are called *flares*.

Common features of juvenile rheumatoid arthritis include joint inflammation, joint contracture, joint damage, and altered growth. Joint inflammation, the most frequent symptom of arthritis, occurs when the lining of the joint swells and becomes overgrown. During an inflammation, the lining also produces too much fluid, resulting in stiffness, pain, warmth, and sometimes redness of the skin that covers the infected area. Because of the pain, many children will try not to move an inflamed joint by keeping it still in a bent position. However, lack of joint movement over a long period of time may cause a deformity, called a joint contracture, as the muscles surrounding the joint become stiff and weak and the tendons that connect the muscles to the bone tighten and shorten.

Joint damage also may occur if the inflammation from the disease is long-lasting and severe. As the lining around the joint swells, friction with the bone damages the joint surfaces. This process, known as joint erosion, is very painful and greatly limits body motion.

In some young people, joint inflammation alters growth by affecting the growth centers in the bones. Bones may become longer, shorter, or thicker than normal as the inflammation speeds or slows the actions of these growth centers. If a large number of these growth centers are damaged, a child may stop growing altogether.

Forms of juvenile rheumatoid arthritis are named for the number of affected joints. For example, *polyarticular* JRA (many joints) is the term used when five or more joints are affected. This form of arthritis usually strikes the small joints of the fingers and hands and often appears in the teenage years. Polyarticular JRA is found more often in girls than in boys. It also can affect the knees, hips, ankles, feet, neck, and jaw; and it often affects the same joint on both sides of the body. The young person with polyarticular JRA may run a low fever or may have rheumatoid nodules on the elbows, soles, or other parts of the body that feel considerable pressure. Because the pain caused by this type of JRA can be severe, the strongest medications for arthritis may be prescribed.

When four or fewer joints are affected, the term used is *pauci-articular* JRA. This form of JRA usually affects a few of the larger joints, such as knees, ankles, or elbows. Pauciarticular JRA usually affects a specific joint on only one side of the body, instead of the same joint on both sides. In addition to affecting the joints, pauciarticular JRA may cause iridocyclitis. *Iridocyclitis* is an eye inflammation that causes red eyes, eye pain, failing vision, and blindness. Often there are no obvious eye symptoms in the early stages of this ailment, and it is important that youngsters have their eyes checked as soon as they are diagnosed with JRA. An early diagnosis by an ophthalmologist will prevent later complications.

The least common form of JRA is *systemic*, meaning affecting the entire body. When a child has systemic JRA, the disease affects the internal organs in addition to the joints. Systemic JRA affects an equal number of boys and girls. Its symptoms include a high fever, rash, swollen joints, and pain. The fever usually rises in the late afternoon or evening, reaching 103°F (40°C) or higher, before returning to normal after a few hours. Often, chills, shaking, and the appearance of pale red spots on the individual's chest and thighs coincide with periods of fever. These fever episodes may last for weeks or months but seldom continue for more than six months.

Joint inflammation problems in systemic JRA may begin at the same time as the fever episodes or may start weeks or months later. In some children, joint pain is severe during a fever and then eases when their temperature returns to normal. For others, joint pain continues long after the feverish period and is a major long-term complication. Internal organ problems associated with systemic JRA include anemia; inflammation of the outer lining of the heart, the heart itself, or the lungs; a high white blood cell count; and enlarged lymph nodes, liver, and spleen.

## Arthritis Treatment and Classroom Responses

Almost all children with arthritis are able to attend a regular school. However, they may need special services. No single pattern of treatment can be established, as childhood arthritis is different in every student. Each mode of therapy has to be individualized according to the student's age, the affected joints, and other disease activity.

At the beginning of the school year, educators should meet with health care professionals to discuss the education and health needs of any affected student. This discussion should include information about medication, the balance between rest and exercise, the wearing of splints or braces, heat or cold therapy, the possibility of surgery, and how teachers and parents will communicate any noticed changes in the student's physical or emotional health. Most types of arthritis in young people cannot be cured. Thus any treatment plan's goal is to keep the arthritis under control by relieving pain, reducing symptoms, preventing deformities, and helping the student better cope with the illness.

Medication is the primary method used by a student with arthritis to suppress and control inflammation and pain. In most treatment programs, the prescribed drug is aspirin. This is the same medication that many people take for headaches; however, people with arthritis take higher doses. Aspirin must be taken in correct dosages on a strict schedule as prescribed by a physician. If the student is not able to tolerate aspirin or if aspirin is not effective, other anti-inflammatory medications, such as hydroxychloroquine, corticosteroids, and liquid gold salt, may be prescribed.

Health care professionals should provide each student's medication schedule to the school. In most cases, medicine should be taken with meals or snacks to prevent stomach upset. It is critical to the child's health that the medication be taken at the prescribed times and in the correct dosage. Arrangements and responsibilities should be stated clearly and understood by the teachers, the student, and the parents. In all cases, the taking of medication should comply with all legal requirements; however, the taking of medication should be as simple and routine as possible.

In some cases, a teacher may need to provide discreet supervision when the student takes medication. This is especially true if the student believes that taking medicine calls attention to the illness and so hides or throws away the medicine. One method suggested by health care providers is for the teacher to establish a routine of subtly checking with the student to be certain that the medication has been taken.

Exercise also is an important part of controlling the effects of arthritis. The student must properly balance exercise and rest. Swollen joints should be rested often and moved gently. For people with arthritis, proper exercise and activity keeps joints mobile and muscles strong and helps to prevent joint stiffness and loss of motion, which may produce deformities and crippling. However, overdoing physical activity for joints and muscles can be detrimental to the student's physical condition.

Students should be encouraged to set their own limits, and teachers should help them avoid overdoing physical activities in an attempt to be accepted. Teachers usually can observe whether a student is overdoing by watching for signs of pain or stiffness, such as grimaces or limping. When these signs appear, students may be pushing themselves too hard and teachers should intervene.

A student's physician should develop guidelines for the school to follow regarding participation in classroom, playground, and physical education activities. These guidelines should be discussed with the parents and the student to be certain that everyone understands any limitations or restrictions. In some cases, the student may need to replace high-impact physical education activities — such as track, soccer, or basketball — with low-impact sports, such as swimming or volleyball, which place less stress on inflamed joints. Other students with arthritis may participate in aggressive sports such as soccer or basketball, though contact sports, such as football, are not recommended. The affected student also may have to wear special protective equipment or train for the sport using special exercises.

In addition to sports and recreational activity, students with arthritis often must perform special therapeutic exercises, or physical therapy. A physical therapist or an occupational therapist measures joint motion and strength and prescribes special exercises that are designed to improve joint mobility and restore lost motion. These exercises must be performed correctly to be effective. Therefore, an important function of the therapist is to instruct the student and the parents in proper exercise techniques. The exercises usually are done at home before school or in the evening; however, if the student needs therapy time during the school day, it should be available. A schedule of required physical therapy should be provided with the medication schedule at the beginning of the school year.

Time required for physical therapy will vary depending on the disease activity. Usually, the student will experience the most severe pain and stiffness in the morning. To ease the stiffness, she or he may take a 10- to 15-minute warm bath or use hot packs or cold treatments before beginning to exercise. If the student is experiencing a flare, physical therapy activities may require extra time and may cause the student to be late to school. Visits to the doctor or physical therapist also may cause absences from school. Teachers must understand that medical appointments and physical therapy are necessary and should make arrangements for the student to make up missed work. When a student misses a class, he or she should be informed about missed information and assignments. Phone calls home and computerized homework hotlines are effective methods for communication. Also, students may be given school work in advance of scheduled appointments.

In some instances, students with arthritis will need to wear custom-made splints or braces to reduce pain, rest inflamed joints, keep joints in their proper position, or prevent or correct deformities. Splints usually are plastic or leather and usually are prescribed to be worn on the arm, wrist, or hand during the night. Sometimes, however, they must be worn during the day and at school. Braces are constructed of metal, plastic, or a cast material and are worn by students who have severe joint damage, muscle weakness, or deformities in their legs. A short class discussion about the purpose of such devices usually will serve to dispel students' curiosity and will help the affected student feel more comfortable.

In rare cases of severe arthritis, a student may require surgery to relieve pain, release a joint contracture, or replace a damaged joint. These students will miss several days or weeks of school. Before the surgery, arrangements should be made to help the student keep up with his or her studies.

## Accommodating Physical Limitations

Arthritis does not affect students' mental abilities, but it may cause physical limitations. Affected students may move slowly or awkwardly or become quickly fatigued. Some students may be unable to walk, hold objects, or perform activities that the other students do effortlessly. Routine activities that some students with arthritis will find difficult include: carrying textbooks or lunch trays, opening lockers, changing clothes for physical education, taking notes, completing tests, walking up and down stairs, or raising a hand to ask a question. Teachers need to be aware of these potential limitations and eliminate physical obstacles to learning. The Individuals with Disabilities Education Act of 1990 was passed to ensure that students with arthritis (or other disabilities) will be educated in the "least restrictive environment" and will receive needed special services. Such services may include physical and occupational therapy, use of a tape recorder or word processor, health monitoring, and special transportation.

Most school systems provide the major required services, but there are times when the simple allowances that make things easier for the student with arthritis are forgotten. An example is prolonged sitting. When a student with JRA sits for a long period of time, the pain and stiffness of arthritis may increase. The teacher should permit the student to move, stand, or do some more physically active task about every 30 minutes so that the joints will not stiffen. Another accommodation may be to schedule the student's classes in rooms that are on the same floor and located near one another. Thus students who have difficulty walking will be better able to arrive on time for each class.

Also, if carrying books is a problem because the weight of the books places stress on sore joints, the proximity of the various classes will shorten the time the books have to be carried. Some schools completely eliminate the problem of carrying books by allowing the student to keep the book for each class in the classroom and providing an extra set of textbooks for use at home. By so doing, the student then has to carry only notebooks and assignment sheets.

As teachers make allowances for the physical limitation of students with arthritis, they should avoid drawing attention to the chronically ill student's physical differences. Self-image is an important part of each student's life, and the teacher plays a major role in shaping that image. Like all students, students with arthritis want to be just like their classmates. The effects of arthritis may limit the realization of that ideal, but their differences should not be magnified by the teacher. Therefore, teachers should attempt to include students with arthritis in as many activities as possible. If the student cannot take an active role in a physical activity, he or she can umpire, keep score, or help in other ways. By making simple allowances and being sensitive to the needs of students with arthritis, teachers can be a positive influence in the student's school experience.

# Chapter Four

# Asthma

About 7 million American adults and 3 million American children under the age of 18 suffer from asthma. It is a common, yet complex lung disease that is most often characterized by a narrowing of the breathing passages. This narrowing may be triggered by various stimuli. Signs of asthma include a chronic cough at rest or after exercise, shortness of breath, tightness in the chest, wheezing, or a crowing or squeaking noise during breathing. Symptoms can be so mild and unobtrusive that many people go undiagnosed. Or the affected individual may suffer an extreme episode, or "asthma attack."

Open airways are necessary for air to enter the lungs and for oxygen to be distributed throughout the body to sustain life. These airways begin with the mouth and nose, followed by the trachea (windpipe), which divides and narrows to the bronchial tubes that, in turn, become increasingly smaller as they branch and go into the lungs. The airways are composed of smooth muscles, mucus membranes that keep breathed air moist, blood vessels, and nerves. All of these structures become involved in the asthmatic process.

For reasons not yet known, the airways in the person with asthma are more sensitive and constrict more easily than in the person without asthma. This characteristic is called hyper-responsiveness or hyperactiveness. An asthmatic response may range from mild to severe and usually is reversible.

Constriction of the airways can be caused by one or more of several factors, such as sporadic contraction of the smooth muscles within the bronchial passages (bronchospasm), increased mucus production, and the swelling or inflammation of the passages and lung tissues. When the tissues lining the airways are irritated, the body's immune system is alerted and rushes to irrigate the area with other fluids, chemicals, and specific cells to fight the irritant. The same occurrence happens when a person scratches his or her skin and the area around the scratch temporarily swells.

Most asthmatic responses are reversible. This means that the changes in the lung tissue that occur with asthma (narrowing and swelling) subside after the asthma episode, and the tissue returns to normal. The lung tissue normally is not damaged with asthma. This characteristic helps distinguish asthma from other lung diseases. For example, a person with emphysema experiences lung tissue damage that is not reversible.

## Types of Asthma

Asthma can be chronic or acute and can occur at any age. If the asthma is controlled, affected individuals can live normal and productive lives. Some young people seem to "outgrow" asthma, but asthmatic symptoms also can return in later years. Chronic asthma produces such symptoms as shortness of breath, wheezing, and coughing. These symptoms result from chronic inflammation of the airways. Students with chronic asthma sometimes cannot tolerate exercise, and they may experience chronic fatigue and weight loss when the symptoms are most severe. In such cases, students may take medicine or use breathing treatments on a daily basis.

The acute episodes, or asthma attacks, can be extremely serious and even life threatening. About 4,300 asthma-related deaths are reported in the United States every year. Some people have no signs of asthma until an attack occurs. Others experience daily symptoms and still can have acute attacks.

36

An asthma attack may be triggered when an irritant, such as mold, dust, pollen, cigarette smoke, smog, or other air pollutant, is breathed in. Or an attack may be precipitated by a cold that affects the lining of the breathing passage and lungs. During the attack, the passage lining swells, narrowing the breathing passage. As the passage swells, a large amount of mucus is secreted, which becomes very thick and sticky and further constricts the airways. This combination of swelling and thick mucus makes it very difficult for the individual to breath. The small amount of air going in and out of the constricted passage makes a whistling, crowing, or wheezing sound. And the individual may cough up some of the mucus.

During a prolonged attack, the affected individual will likely be breathless and may be unable to talk. His or her neck muscles will appear to be tight, and breathing may become so difficult that the individual's chest skin sucks in around the ribs when breathing (chest retractions). His or her lips and nails may become gray or blue in color.

As the attack progresses, inability to breath may lead to anxiety or panic, which may increase the severity of the attack. Of course, asthma attacks vary in severity and duration. And people with recurring asthma usually take prescribed medicine to prevent attacks and to help them if one should occur. But severe attacks require emergency treatment.

## Controlling Asthma

Helping the student who is living with asthma requires a team effort. Regular communications with the medical team will keep teachers and parents up to date on the latest medicines and treatments. Teachers, as well as parents and the young people themselves, must understand that environmental factors play a significant role in triggering asthmatic reactions. Minimizing such factors at home and in school may be an important part of the treatment for asthma. For example, teachers and administrators should consider removing loose rugs and cleaning carpets and drapes that trap dust and other allergens. Teachers should be cautious about allowing animals into the classroom or keeping a rabbit, gerbil, or other classroom pet. In older schools or buildings in which air circulation may be poor, an air filtration unit might be installed in the classroom.

Cold air also can trigger an asthma episode. Therefore, teachers need to be aware of their students' conditions before sending students with asthma for outdoor recess in cold weather.

Medicine to control asthma may be administered in many ways: nasal sprays, aerosol inhalers, compressor-driven breathing treatments, pills or capsules, and liquids that are swallowed. Injections often are used to reverse asthma attacks, and regular "allergy shots" may be used to desensitize persons with asthma to certain environmental triggers, such as allergies to grasses. The routines for allergy shots vary from every few days to monthly. The affected student's physician will determine the type of medicine and the treatment routine. Teachers and administrators need to be aware of the regimen in order to facilitate its implementation.

Educators should be aware of the major types of medicine that are used in the treatment of asthma:

*Corticosteroids* are a large group of drugs that are effective in reducing inflammation and overreaction by the airways. They often are prescribed for students who have asthma. When taken in a pill form, these drugs sometimes produce harsh side effects, such as stomach upsets and, in some cases, stomach ulcers. When these drugs are delivered by means of an inhaler, the side effects are minimized and the positive effects of the drugs are achieved more rapidly.

*Bronchodilators* are another group of drugs that are used to open the airway. They work by relaxing the constricted smooth muscles of the airway. Children with chronic asthma usually take home nebulizer treatments. A nebulizer is a compressor-driven breathing machine that forces medicated air into the user's lungs. The liquid bronchodilator is placed into the nebulizer, and the user breathes the medicated air for a specified period of time or until the medicine has been completely used. The nebulizer helps the user breathe in the medicine more deeply than may be possible by using an aerosol inhaler.

Parents should be able to arrange for a nebulizer to be kept in the health room at the school for the child to use with supervision on days when the child's asthma is troublesome. If a school nurse is not on site, the person assigned to oversee the health room can be trained easily to use the nebulizer and assess its effectiveness.

*Cromolyn* is another effective medicine used to decrease the airway's response to environmental triggers. It can be administered in an inhaler or a nasal spray, but it is best used on a continual basis to prevent asthma attacks. It is not effective once an asthma attack has begun.

Educators can assist in the management of the student's chronic illness by observing the student during school activities and in various settings and noting any changes in the student's reaction to his or her illness and the effectiveness of treatment, for example, whether certain medicines act quickly or slowly and how the student feels after treatment or medication. These observations should be an important part of the communication between school and home and with the medical team.

## School Responses and Responsibilities

Children spend about seven hours a day in school, which makes the school a major environment in students' lives. School personnel need to ensure that the school environment will not cause problems for students with asthma. Furthermore, should a student experience an asthma episode, he or she needs to be assured of prompt, appropriate care.

The first step toward effectively managing students' asthma conditions is good communication among the individuals who make up each individual student's health care team — parents, the student, medical professionals (including the school nurse), teachers, and administrators. This team should meet at the start of each school year and then meet periodically during the year to update information if the student's condition changes.

School personnel also need to know specifically how each chronically ill student's parents want the school to handle emergencies. Today, many parents of chronically ill youngsters carry electronic pagers to be used for just such emergencies. But notifying parents may not be a priority in an emergency. It may be more important to have accurate information about the student's medical condition close to hand. The Asthma and Allergy Foundation of America supplies an excellent resource for schools, called the "Student Asthma Action Card," on which information provided by the parents can be documented in an efficient format. Ready access to such information is important for teachers and administrators so that they can respond quickly and appropriately in the event of a medical emergency.

Day-to-day management of asthma is equally important. Most children with asthma are on various treatment and medication regimens, whose side effects can become a problem for the student at school. Side effects may include headache, hand tremors, fatigue, and stomach pain. All of these reactions can affect the student's ability to learn. When side effects interfere with learning, teachers should inform the student's parents. The parents and medical personnel may decide that the medicine or treatment routine can be modified. Likewise, parents should be asked to let their child's teacher know if the child has had a sleepless night because of asthma or if the child should drink more fluids in order to help thin mucus secretions. Good communication between home and school will allow teachers to better understand chronically ill students' conditions and to create environments where students with asthma can feel comfortable and be able to effectively control the asthma.

Even with effective maintenance and good communication, some students will miss school because of asthma. The well-informed teacher will not send a student with mild asthma symptoms home unnecessarily. However, sometimes a youngster will use his or her asthma as an excuse not to attend school or to get out of some activity. Frequent, direct communication between parents and teachers can be useful in discouraging this behavior.

Following are some specific potential problem areas for students with asthma:

*Physical education* can present problems for the student living with asthma. Before the student begins physical education activities or signs up for an after-school sport, the student's doctor should send information to the school or coach concerning any physical limitations related to chronic illness. The physician also should be asked to outline what to do to prevent asthma episodes and how to control them if they should occur. Coaches need to know what medicines the student should take before or after exercise. It will be important to prevent exercise-induced asthma. By understanding each chronically ill student's needs and limitations, the school can facilitate the student's participation in physical programs.

*Poorly ventilated areas* can cause problems for the student with asthma. Often school physical plants are old. Dust and chalk dust can be irritants. Allergens from classroom pets and molds can lurk in carpets and closets. Proper classroom ventilation is essential for the student with asthma, as is attention to cleaning and maintenance. Areas that need special attention to ventilation and cleaning include science and art classrooms, where fumes from chemicals, paints, and other materials may trigger asthma episodes. Students with severe asthma may need to avoid such areas altogether.

Lack of air conditioning may cause problems for students with asthma during the summer months. However, air conditioners with poorly maintained filters that allow allergens, such as mold, to be spread in classrooms can be just as troublesome.

*Food allergies* can be another source of problems for students with asthma. Both certain foods and some food preservatives may trigger asthma episodes. Potential problems in this area should be discussed with cafeteria managers and teachers who may permit students to eat snacks or special treats in the classroom from time to time.

*Colds and other contagious illnesses* that students bring to school can create more serious problems for students with asthma. Teachers who are aware of this potential can discuss and promote good hygiene for all students. For the student with asthma, nasal congestion and ear infections also can interfere with hearing. Teachers should be alert to hearing problems, which may be evident through changes in the student's behavior, such as lack of attentiveness or difficulty following verbal directions.

In conclusion, asthma may or may not affect the chronically ill student's school life, depending on the severity of his or her condition. Educators who are well-informed and observant can develop school environments that limit potential problems. And they will be ready to respond effectively when emergencies arise.

# Chapter Five

# Cancer

The term *cancer* applies to a group of diseases, each with its own name, prognosis, and treatment. Every person's body occasionally makes abnormal cells, but an efficient immune system usually destroys and removes the abnormalities. Cancer is diagnosed when abnormal body cells begin to take over and replace normal cells. In most cancers, the abnormal cells also invade surrounding tissues and can travel to other areas in the body. Some types of cancer progress slowly, other rapidly. Left unchecked, most types of cancer eventually will cause death.

Scientists do not know what triggers the growth of abnormal cells, but they do know that certain environmental and familial factors make adults more prone to develop cancer. The contributing factors for many childhood and adolescent cancers are even less clear. Much research is being performed in the areas of cytology, immunology, genetics, and environmental medicine to determine the causes and to find cures for cancer.

Some childhood cancers have a survival rate up to 90%. One in every 1,000 young people who reach age 20 is a survivor of childhood cancer. These dramatic survival rates are a result of advances in anticancer drug therapy (or chemotherapy), surgical techniques, and radiation therapy. Advances have been made in handling the toxic side effects of many of the drugs used in chemotherapy, such as ulcerations in the mouth and gastrointestinal tract, nausea and vomiting, and bone marrow suppression, which leaves a person weak and susceptible to infection or bleeding. By controlling such side effects, doctors are able to more aggressively treat cancer in children.

The most common types of childhood cancer are leukemias, followed by brain tumors, lymphomas, and other solid tumors, such as tumors of the kidneys and bones. Early diagnosis increases the chance of survival, but it often is difficult because early cancer signs can imitate other problems, such as mononucleosis or juvenile rheumatoid arthritis. Once cancer is suspected, the young person usually is referred to a pediatric cancer center for diagnosis and treatment.

A number of cancers are incurable. Thus, in many cases, the treatment goal is to achieve remission. When a person is "in remission," no cancerous cells are detectable. The longer the remission, the closer the person comes to being cured. If the cancer recurs after a period of remission, the patient is said to have "relapsed." When this happens, treatment is begun again. Students with cancer may be in and out of school, both because of remission and relapse and because of the nature of treatment.

Following are descriptions of four types of cancers that affect young people, their treatment, and how teachers can help make participation in school a good experience for affected students.

## Types of Cancer

*Leukemias* are cancers of the blood-producing tissues, such as the bone marrow. They account for one-third of all childhood cancers. Acute lymphoblastic leukemia (ALL) accounts for 75% of all childhood leukemias. Other leukemias include: acute non-lymphocytic leukemia (15% to 20% of childhood leukemias; 40% survival rate), acute myelogenous leukemia (also 40% survival rate), and chronic leukemias (less than 5% of childhood leukemias; less than 30% survival rate after 5 years).

Treatment of ALL has become a true success story in modern medicine. Over the past 45 years, ALL has moved from being fatal within two to three months after diagnosis to a survival rate of more than 60%.

ALL is diagnosed most often in children about four years old. It is more common in whites than blacks and more common in prepubescent males than females. Prognosis is extremely poor for infants under 12 months old and poorer for males than females. Common relapse sites are the central nervous system (the brain and spinal cord) and the testicles. Thus, even after treatment has achieved remission, additional maintenance or continuation therapy is required to take care of potential relapse sites.

The initial evaluation of ALL requires sophisticated laboratory techniques to derive accurate cellular and immunological information in order to best treat the cancer. Treatment of ALL is divided into four regimens: remission induction, central nervous system (CNS) preventive therapy, consolidation treatment, and maintenance therapy. Treatment approaches will vary for each case, but the basic treatment goals will be the same.

Remission induction therapy is the use of drugs designed to inhibit the growth or spread of a cancer. Chemotherapy drugs are specific to the cancer cell cycle in which the cancer cell can be destroyed. Chemotherapy also targets fast-growing cells. Therefore, side effects, such as hair loss (hair also is produced by fast-growing cells), are common. Failure of induction therapy to produce remission is rare, occurring in less than 5% of the cancer patients. Improved supportive care to reverse the toxic side effects of chemotherapy has decreased mortality from the induction therapy to less than 3%.

The recognition of central nervous system involvement in acute lymphoblastic leukemia and the commencement of CNS preventive therapy have eliminated a major obstacle to successful treatment. Researchers have discovered that undetected leukemic cells often reside in the central nervous system and are protected from drugs administered during induction therapy by the blood-brain barrier. In CNS treatment, chemotherapy is directed into the spinal fluid along with radiation therapy to the brain and spinal cord.

Immediately after a remission is achieved, consolidation therapy begins. This is a period of intensified treatment designed to make certain that the cancer cells have been destroyed. Consolidation therapy has improved the survival rates of children who are particularly at risk of relapse. Maintenance therapy then follows for an individualized length of time. Young people who receive maintenance therapy on a continual, uninterrupted schedule experience longer remissions. Investigators have demonstrated that the optimal period for maintenance therapy is about three years. In order to improve prognosis and minimize permanent side effects, researchers continually are investigating new drugs and treatment protocols, as well as attempting to understand the causes and ways to prevent leukemia.

*Lymphomas* are cancers of the circulating immune system or lymphatic system. The immune system is one of the body's strategic defenses against invading organisms, such as viruses and bacteria. It is made up of various cells that have specific functions. Lymph nodes throughout the body and the spleen are the key points for potential cancer. Because of the circulation, most lymphomas are generalized throughout the body and mimic the migration of the normal immune cell they replace.

The most common lymphomas are non-Hodgkin's lymphoma and Hodgkin's lymphoma. These two diagnoses are broad terms; various specific types of cancer occur in both types. The precise diagnosis is associated with the type of cell that is abnormal.

Lymphomas account for about 10% to 13% of all childhood cancers, but they are less common in children than adults. Lymphomas rarely occur before age 5. They tend to be more common in males than females. Symptoms of lymphatic cancer can include fatigue, loss of appetite, weight loss, unexplained fever, swollen and painless lymph nodes in the neck and shoulders, and night sweats. The differences between childhood and adult lymphomas are a result of age-related differences in the immune system.

The treatment of choice in all lymphomas is chemotherapy. It is common to receive combination therapy similar to that used in cases of leukemia. In lymphomas, a tumor usually is involved that most often lies in the mid-chest cavity region. Chemotherapy is used to break down the tumor, and the child is closely monitored to prevent complications that can arise from the tumor breaking down. Treatment of Hodgkin's disease also includes radiation therapy, and usually the patient's spleen is removed.

In recent years, the survival rates for persons with lymphomas have greatly improved. Patients with non-Hodgkin's lymphoma are cured in about two-thirds of the cases, and people with Hodgkin's lymphoma have a 96% success rate of being cured.

*Brain tumors* are the second most common type of cancer in young people. Most occur in children older than ten. However, about 10% of all brain tumors occur in children under age two; and these are the children most likely to suffer from the severest complications of treatment. Tumors in children also have a different origin from brain tumors in adults. Currently, many studies are being done in the areas of cytology, immunology, genetics, and environmental medicine to differentiate causes of tumors and to discover how best to intervene and prevent the tumors from occurring. Symptoms in children with brain tumors include headaches, varying degrees of seizures, paralysis on one side, loss of senses (hearing, smell, touch) on one side, or visual deficits.

As with other cancers, treatment of brain tumors has vastly improved in the last 15 years. Although neurosurgical removal is still the treatment of choice, brain tumors are being removed with greater success than in the past because of modern highly sophisticated scanning and imaging technology. Radiation therapy technology also has become more highly specific. Many inoperable tumors now can be treated with a laser-like stream of radiation. Radiation and surgery often are preceded by chemotherapy.

A patient's prognosis is determined by the age of the child and the type and extent of the tumor. Complications from the cancer treatment may damage surrounding brain tissues and cause severe to mild deficits in the child's ability to function. However, most long-term survivors are free from any disabling neurological deficits.

*Other solid tumors* include sarcomas, retinoblastomas, liver tumors, tumors of the kidneys and testicles, and endocrine tumors.

A sarcoma is a malignant solid tumor arising from the cells that evolve into supportive tissue, such as muscle, cartilage, and bone. Rhabdomyosarcoma (RMS) and undifferentiated sarcoma (UDS) are the most common types of muscle cancer found in young people under age 15. These forms of cancer can metastasize, or spread from the local area of the tumor to other areas of the body, such as the lymph tissues, lungs, bone marrow, and bones. All of these areas must be studied thoroughly at the time of diagnosis. Currently three methods are used in treating sarcomas: surgical removal, radiation therapy, and chemotherapy. This combination offers the best chance of survival. Chemotherapy usually is continued for one to two years after diagnosis to prevent a relapse. Complications of treatment can affect the child for life, such as learning to live with an amputated limb.

Ewing's sarcoma, the next most common type of bone cancer in youth, commonly occurs during adolescence. It is rare before age 5 or after age 30. The most common metastatic site for this cancer is the lungs, followed by other bone areas and bone marrow. Approximately 50% of all patients have metastasis at diagnosis. The most common symptom is pain and swelling at the affected bone or region. Fatigue, loss of appetite, weight loss, intermittent fever, and malaise also may be present when there is metastatic disease. The most common bone sites are the pelvis, humerus, and femur, although it may arise in any bone.

The goal of treating Ewing's sarcoma — as well as other bone cancers, such as osteosarcoma and fibrosarcoma — is to preserve as much function as possible along with permanent local control, treatment, and prevention. Chemotherapy is initiated after a biopsy report is confirmed. This allows the treatment team to evaluate the tumor's response to the chemotherapy before it is removed in order to achieve the most effective follow up treatment. Often, a tumor that cannot be removed surgically (called unresectable) becomes resectable after chemotherapy has begun to destroy it.

Other more common solid tumors of the young include the following:

- Retinoblastomas, a malignant tumor of the retina in the eyes;
- Liver tumors, which pose particular treatment challenges;
- Wilm's tumors of the kidneys;
- Tumors of the testicles; and
- Endocrine tumors, such as tumors of the thyroid.

Regardless of where tumors arise or how they are treated, the affected student's challenges in treatment and living with cancer flow into the daily routines of school. Such issues as quality of life, growth and development, and educational and social needs are as important for the student with cancer as for his or her healthy peers. Therefore, it is important for the teacher to remember that the school setting often is viewed as a haven of normalcy for the student with cancer. Academic participation during this time can help the student to gain satisfaction and feel productive when other aspects of his or her life are proving to be a challenge.

## The Teacher's Role

For teachers to effectively address the needs of students undergoing cancer treatment or returning to school following intensive treatment, they must have information. Often parents are their best source. Teachers should know the type of cancer for which the student is being treated and the form of treatment. This information will help the teacher plan activities and assignments that are appropriate to the student's ability to study during treatment or recovery.

Teachers should be aware that the patient undergoing chemotherapy is particularly susceptible to infections. The patient's immune system will be closely monitored by the medical team, and the student will not be allowed to return to school until it appears to be safe for him or her to do so. However, exposure to diseases, such as shingles, chicken pox, or measles, are particularly dangerous for the student. The teacher should immediately report any actual or suspected exposures to the parents. It may be possible to prevent serious complications if the exposure is reported immediately.

Although medical emergencies in the classroom are rare for students with cancer, the potential for medical emergencies may exist and should be discussed with the parents or medical team. Minor medical problems, such as nausea and headaches, should be treated as they would be treated in other students, but any persistent problems should be reported.

Many students with cancer experience frequent absences for medical reasons, are able to participate only in limited physical activities, and may feel socially isolated. Well-planned re-entry strategies can effectively overcome these negative aspects. The school nurse, the student's physician, the school counselor, and the social worker will be important sources of information and guidance for the teacher — and for parents, who may be prone to overindulge the affected child or be overprotective to the child's detriment. Teachers also should remember that students with cancer are growing and developing just as their peers are. Thus chronically ill students also should participate in routine health screenings, such as vision and hearing exams.

The teacher also needs to know what the student knows about the illness. Occasionally a family will choose to not tell the child about the extent of the illness. On the other hand, many students, especially adolescents, choose to be a part of the discussion and will decide what they want their classmates to know. Different families handle living with cancer differently; there is no standard. Many parents, seeing their child handle a life-threatening illness, will experience grief and will express grief and anger. Teachers need to understand that such expressions and feelings are normal, and they should not take the expressions personally. The best approach to working with students and families in medical crises is a team approach. Often psychologists and social workers can suggest effective approaches for working with a "difficult" family.

Working with students undergoing cancer treatment may be challenging. Such students need to be accepted by their peers, just as other students do. But the student with cancer also is struggling in other ways. For such students, cancer is a part of their lives that must not be overlooked. At the same time, focusing solely on the cancer can obliterate other important aspects of life. Therefore, the teacher's challenge is to help the affected student to attain a balance. Some concessions will need to be made because of the illness and its treatment, but students should be helped to maintain their self-image through involvement in class-room activities on as equal a basis with their peers as possible.

This means that teachers should avoid becoming overprotective. They should appropriately discipline affected students and hold them responsible for reasonable academic expectations. Having lower standards for students with cancer lowers affected students' self-esteem, raises barriers to pride in their accomplishment, and may lead to resentment from their classmates. Evaluation criteria should be the same for all students. However, assignment deadlines for the student with cancer may have to be adjusted because of treatment schedules and recovery periods.

When students are absent for long periods, classroom teachers must maintain frequent communication with homebound teachers in order to help the students keep up with assignments. Doing so will allow the affected students to continue to feel as though they are part of the class, and it will make their re-entry smoother.

## How Other Classmates Can Help

No student's illness should be discussed with anyone outside the health care team without the parents' permission. Some school systems require prior written permission before an illness such as cancer can be discussed in class. The content and manner of the discussion should be circumscribed by the wishes of the student and his or her family. Any class discussion also should be suited to the age of the students.

Given these conditions, however, many affected students and their classmates will benefit from discussing a chronic illness. Classmates who better understand their peer's medical condition and treatment often can help the student to cope better with his or her illness.

Teachers may be able to use discussions about a specific student's illness to teach related information. For example, a class might study a unit on cancer. Finding information and resources could help the affected student learn more about his or her own illness.

Another effective way for other students to learn about a student's cancer is to listen to a member of the affected student's health care team. The teacher and the affected student might invite this person to visit the classroom and discuss care and treatment with the class. In many cases, this type of presentation and discussion also allows the affected student to respond to questions from classmates. Many students with cancer want to talk about their illness and willingly respond to questions from their peers. Openness of this sort also can blunt any teasing from classmates. Students sometimes tease or ridicule chronically ill students because they do not understand these students' illnesses or because the affected students seem to garner more of the teacher's attention.

For younger children, in particular, stories and role playing provide constructive ways of coping and dealing with feelings. But it is important to remember that if a student with cancer was a "loner" before the cancer, that characteristic probably will not change because of the cancer. When the student is inclined to avoid other people, encouraging acceptance by classmates becomes particularly difficult. Students with these personalities are particularly prone to feelings of isolation, and so it is doubly important for the teacher to cue into the emotional needs of these students and to be supportive.

When chronically ill students are absent for an extended period, teachers also should help them stay in touch with their classmates. Visits to the hospital or the home and telephone calls by classmates can be arranged. Doing so not only helps the student feel a part of the class, it reduces anxiety in classmates who may be wondering about their absent friend. The teacher can be an important facilitator in preventing the student with cancer from feeling forgotten.

## When Treatment Fails

Even with much improved survival rates, cancer often is a terminal illness. The final stages of cancer are emotionally painful for everyone. However, a few simple measures can be helpful to everyone. One is accommodating the affected student so that he or she can attend school for as long as possible. An hour or two each day can be very rewarding for the student with cancer and for the other students in class. Many students and teachers realize how precious life, time, and relationships are during this critical period.

When a student dies, his or her classmates may express their grief in a variety of ways, ranging from indifference to open crying. Teachers should acknowledge their own and their students' feelings of loss. No attempt should be made to "control" the grieving process. Each individual must be allowed to work through emotions and find comfort and resolution. Questions about death, particularly from young students, should be dealt with simply and honestly.

A memorial service can be helpful for the students to come to terms with their friend's death. Older students who were particularly close to the deceased student may be allowed to attend the funeral service. Classmates may want to create their own memorial through some activity, such as planting a tree or garden in memory of the student or raising funds for a special piece of equipment for the school. The family and siblings of the deceased student often appreciate these expressions.

In conclusion, the experience of working with young students living with cancer can be rewarding and enriching. Often, working with students who have cancer brings a new perspective on life. The teacher may draw from the experience a sharpened sense of value and purpose. Students with cancer may offer valuable experiences and memories that will continue to touch the lives of students and teachers for many years.

# Chapter Six

# Cystic Fibrosis

Cystic fibrosis (CF) is an inherited, chronic disorder that affects some 30,000 children and young adults. It is the most common, fatal genetic disease in the United States.

CF affects the sweat glands, the bronchi of the lungs, the pancreas, and the mucus-secreting glands of the small intestines. The symptoms of this disease include a high concentration of sodium and chloride (salts) in the sweat, abnormal secretions of mucus that are particularly thick and sticky, and abnormal food absorption and bowel elimination. Other common symptoms are salty-tasting skin, persistent coughing or wheezing, chronic lung infections such as pneumonia, excessive appetite with poor weight gain, and greasy, bulky, foul-smelling stools. Parents who discover a salty taste upon kissing their child should consider further investigation by a physician.

CF usually is diagnosed in young children; the average age at diagnosis is three. When the Cystic Fibrosis Foundation was formed in 1955, the average age of survival was not much beyond age 5. However, today individuals with CF can live well into adulthood. Mortality usually is related to severe lung infections that are resistant to current antibiotics. Advances in research and medication over the last few years have increased the life expectancy of those who contract this disease.

The CF gene was discovered in 1989, and since then the pace of research has increased dramatically. One in 20 Americans carries the CF gene. Therefore, when two people who are carriers of the gene conceive, each offspring has a 25% chance of contracting CF. Carriers of the gene have no symptoms and may not know that they are carriers until an offspring with CF is born.

## Treatment of CF

Currently, six universities are being funded to research gene therapy for CF patients. One therapy being tested is a virus shuttle. Researchers use a nasal spray to deliver healthy, laboratory-engineered genes into the lung tissue by means of engineered viruses. The viruses act as shuttles to carry the healthy genes to the correct locations in the breathing passages and lungs. This gene treatment has been used to repair defective CF cells for a few weeks. At this time the federal Food and Drug Administration (FDA) has approved a two-part protocol in which repeated doses of gene therapy will be administered to a total of 40 adults with CF. Scientists believe that gene therapy may be a promising answer for people with CF.

Patients with CF experience great difficulty with mucus in their breathing passages and lungs. Coughing is the primary way to clear the airways. People with CF are taught to cough often and effectively to help remove the thick mucus. Excess mucus provides a breeding ground for bacteria to grow and cause dangerous illnesses. For these reasons, the individual with CF should avoid taking cough suppressants. Drug companies are developing new drugs that thin the tenacious mucus so that it is easier to cough up in order to prevent bacteria growth.

The treatment of CF depends on the individual, how far the illness has progressed, and which organs are involved. The daily medical routines can be rigorous. Many CF patients take antibiotics to prevent infections. Pancreatic enzymes, taken in a pill form, also can aid digestion and prevent malnutrition.

When the lungs are involved, it is imperative that the patient have what is called "pulmonary toileting." This procedure involves assisting the patient to remove excess mucus through "chest physical therapy," a procedure that consists of postural drainage along with cupping and clapping. Postural drainage is when the patient lies on one side with the head lower than the feet. Gravity helps the patient cough up excess mucus. A second person, usually a parent in the case of children, cups his or her hands and claps the back and chest vigorously and rhythmically. The cupping of the hands prevents the procedure from being painful and also allows more vibration to go through the chest to loosen secretions. Still in the downward position, the child then coughs deeply to bring up the mucus. In many cases, this has to be done twice a day.

In addition to the chest physical therapy, patients often need to use a compressor-driven nebulizer to deliver antibiotics or bronchodilators into the lungs. This breathing treatment not only helps open up the airways but also helps reduce the chance of infections. Some CF patients also need to be given intravenous antibiotics to prevent infections and the lung damage that can occur with repeated infections. Although these treatments usually can be done on an outpatient basis, they may result in students missing all or parts of several school days.

CF patients also may experience digestive problems. Acids and enzymes are vital to digest food. A person with CF has so much mucus that it blocks the digestive system and prevents the pancreatic enzymes from reaching the small intestines, where the majority of digestion takes place. Without taking extra enzymes, the body cannot digest food properly and the person will become malnourished. Indeed, infants and young children with CF often are first diagnosed because they fail to gain sufficient weight. Extra digestive enzymes taken with each meal and snack and a high-calorie meal plan help the body absorb the nutrients it needs.

Sometimes CF also damages the pancreas, and so it is not uncommon for the CF child to develop diabetes. The combination of CF and diabetes presents particular difficulties and challenges for all involved in the youngster's care because of problems with absorption of nutrients. Close observation of the student and frequent communication with parents and the medical team are extremely important in such cases.

## CF and Teacher Responsibilities

It is important for teachers to remember that CF is not contagious and that it affects each patient differently. They should not generalize about the health status, physical or emotional, of students with CF. Some students with CF will be able to attend class regularly; others will be able to attend for only part of the day; still others may be in such poor health that they will need to be home-schooled or taught by a homebound teacher.

The affected student's parents usually are a good resource and can help the teacher identify the student's strengths and areas of difficulty. The meeting at the beginning of the year between parents and teachers is vital so that the student can fit into the school environment. The "fit" will depend on meeting both the academic and health needs of the chronically ill student. And those needs may change as the year progresses if the nature or severity of the student's illness changes.

Students with CF often take many doses of medicine; some students must take as many as 25 pills each day. Other students with CF may periodically need to use a compressor-driven nebulizer in the school health room. None of the standard medicines for treating CF produce side effects that should interfere with the student's school performance. However, teachers should realize that the stress of being ill may affect academic performance, in addition to the sometimes frequent absences that will take up valuable learning time.

Teachers need to understand that some students will prefer to take their medicine in private. Other students cannot be trusted or are too young to take their medicines unsupervised. Therefore, a clear plan must be developed to ensure that medication is timely, accurate, and consistent. School policies will govern whether medicines are kept in the classroom under the teacher's supervision or in the school health room supervised by a nurse and how medicines are monitored and administered.

Such policies also should include information about handling emergencies. CF usually does not produce a medical emergency.

However, an emergency can arise if a student with CF experiences a breathing obstruction. A mucus plug can cause an asthma-like episode. Such an episode might result from the student's failure to follow a treatment routine, or it might signal the onset of a lung infection. In such an event, emergency assistance should be summoned.

## Exercise and Sports for Students with CF

Physical activity is particularly beneficial for students with CF. Exercise and sports should be encouraged. Running and playing hard helps expand the lungs and helps the child cough up excess mucus secretions. Coughing clears the airways and removes matter in which bacteria grow. However, some students may not have enough stamina to play hard. These children should be encouraged to do as much as they can and then take frequent rests.

Only part of the benefit from sports and exercise is physical. Another benefit is psychological. Playing hard also increases self-esteem and helps build social maturity.

In conclusion, an understanding and appreciation of the rigors involved with keeping cystic fibrosis under control will help the teacher to develop an optimal learning environment for students with CF. This environment will address chronically ill students' health needs in the fullest sense — that is, both physical and psychological health. By developing a positive therapeutic relationship, the teacher also will be better able to develop a positive instructional relationship with students who have cystic fibrosis.

# Chapter Seven

# Diabetes Mellitus

Diabetes mellitus is the seventh leading cause of death in the United States and a major cause of heart attacks, strokes, blindness, nontraumatic amputations, and kidney failure. The hallmark of the illness is high blood glucose (sugar), which is caused by a deficiency of or resistance to one's own insulin.

Insulin is the hormone produced in the beta cells (or islet cells) of the pancreas. This hormone enables the body to use food, as glucose, for growth and energy. Glucose comes from the breakdown of the foods that we eat as well as from glycogen, muscle, and fat stores within body tissue. It is required by the body's cells for fuel in order for the body to function normally. If insufficient insulin is present in the blood stream or the body resists using its own insulin, then glucose cannot move from the bloodstream into the cells. Thus the individual's cells starve, and his or her blood sugar level gets higher and higher. High blood sugar levels over a long period of time will negatively affect every major organ system of the body.

There are two main types of diabetes mellitus. The first is called insulin-dependent diabetes mellitus (IDDM or Type I). This is the type of diabetes most often seen in young people. It usually occurs before age 20 and rarely occurs after age 30. The second type of diabetes mellitus is called noninsulin-dependent diabetes (NIDDM or Type II). This second type of diabetes most commonly occurs in individuals older than 40. If it does occur in a young person, that individual most often is an obese adolescent with a family history of diabetes.

IDDM is not contagious, and there is nothing a person or the family could have done to prevent it. People who have IDDM are required to take insulin injections for the rest of their lives. The insulin injections are intended to imitate the body's normal release of insulin from the pancreas to maintain a normal blood glucose level. By balancing insulin dosage, meal planning, and exercise, it is possible to prevent both high blood glucose levels (hyperglycemia) and low blood glucose levels (hypoglycemia).

The process of beta cell destruction begins months or years before diabetes presents itself. Such cell destruction is described as an autoimmune process, meaning that the body begins to destroy its own beta cells. In order for IDDM to develop, the individual first must have the genetic tendency to develop diabetes. Scientific research has revealed that certain tissue types make some people more prone to diabetes than others. Currently, researchers are in the process of identifying people with these tissue types and attempting to prevent IDDM if the autoimmune process has begun. Second, the individual must be exposed to an environmental "trigger," such as a virus, which starts the autoimmune process. When about 90% of the beta cells have been destroyed, the affected individual will show symptoms of diabetes.

## Observable Symptoms

The student with diabetes may exhibit several symptoms of the disease. For example, as the blood gets thick with glucose, fluid inside the body cells shifts to the bloodstream. The kidneys, being the body's fluid regulators, attempt to adjust the fluids in the body and maintain a normal state. However, like a lake rising against a dam, the extra fluid, glucose, and electrolytes (sodium, potassium, phosphorus, etc.) spill into the urine. As the fluids continue to spill and the body begins to dry out, the thirst center in the brain is triggered and tells the person to drink. Thus some of the first signs of high blood sugar are increased thirst and increased urination.

In many instances, parents have reported that bed wetting was the first sign of diabetes exhibited by their children. As the autoimmune process continues, the affected individual will become weak and hungry. His or her body cells are starving and crying out for more fuel. The liver then responds and begins to break down other sources for fuel, such as fat and muscle. Therefore, in this stage the person begins to lose weight, even if he or she is eating a great deal.

The breakdown of fat presents another problem: ketones. This byproduct of the breakdown of fatty acids causes stomach cramps, nausea, and vomiting and makes the affected individual's body go into an acid state. Ketones often can be smelled on the person's breath. The acetone odor is similar to smell of overripe fruit or fingernail polish remover. This acidosis, along with the dehydration, causes severe illness marked by deep, rapid breathing. Most individuals are at this stage when they are diagnosed. If left untreated, the individual with these symptoms will slip into a coma and die within a few days or weeks.

Similar symptoms also can occur in the second type of diabetes, NIDDM. When this type is seen in a young person, some health care professionals refer to it as MODY (maturity onset diabetes of youth). The problem in NIDDM is not lack of insulin, but insulin resistance, which is the body's inability to use the insulin it produces. Insulin resistance is directly proportional to the amount of body fat. The heavier the person is, the more insulin resistance that person will have. As in the case of their older counterparts, young people with NIDDM will likely be sensitive to weight loss. Often they can go into a remission with some weight loss and a few lifestyle changes, such as adopting a healthier diet and engaging in more physical activities. In fact, many young people can be treated with diet and exercise alone. However, some will require diet and exercise plus medicine to lower insulin resistance or insulin injections.

## Managing Diabetes at School

People who have IDDM or NIDDM should monitor their blood sugar several times a day, but many health care professionals do not require young people to monitor at school. Daily management of diabetes makes many students feel different from their healthy peers in the first place. Monitoring at school, even using the latest one-step monitoring technology, often adds to the perceived "stigma."

Each student with diabetes will have individual social, psychological, and medical needs. Thus the decision whether to monitor blood sugar during the day at school will vary. But in all cases, teachers need to help students feel comfortable enough to communicate about their diabetes-related needs. The recently diagnosed student with diabetes may be learning how to recognize the feelings associated with low blood sugar, and so the teacher must be alert to signs and symptoms and must know how to respond.

During school hours, the most common times for low blood sugar reactions are just before lunch and in the middle of the afternoon. Insulin that was taken before breakfast will be working best to lower the student's blood sugar at these times. Therefore, most young people should have a mid-morning and a mid-afternoon snack to prevent low blood sugar episodes. Parents should provide information about the type of snacks their children should eat, and in most cases parents will be responsible for providing those snacks. A typical mid-morning or mid-afternoon snack might be two or three peanut-butter crackers and a small piece of fruit.

Snacks and school lunches should include mainly healthy, high-fiber, low-fat foods. Each student with diabetes should follow a personalized meal plan developed by a registered dietitian. Compliance with the meal plan is often the most difficult part of the diabetes regimen, but it is essential for good diabetes management. Students with diabetes may eat foods with sugar. However, concentrated sugars should be limited to special occasions. For example, a student with diabetes may eat cake and ice cream during a classroom party, but the student's parents should be informed in advance in order to make meal and insulin adjustments.

A number of specific problems may arise because of school activities. These potential problems merit brief discussion:

*Physical Education and Exercise.* The timing of the physical education or exercise periods — including active recess — and lunch are major management issues for the student with diabetes. Therefore, parents and school officials should discuss the student's class schedule before the start of the school year.

The optimal time to schedule a physical education class for the student with diabetes is right after lunch. Like insulin, exercise lowers the blood sugar. A young person often needs extra food with extra exercise. If a physical education period falls during the morning, a snack before or after the class is necessary to prevent a low blood sugar episode before lunch. The snack could be as simple as a small box of raisins to eat while changing classes. If the student does not eat a well-balanced breakfast in the morning, the snack may need to be heavier, such as peanut-butter crackers and juice. If lunch is scheduled between 10:30 and 11:30, the student may be able to skip the mid-morning snack if there is no exercise class.

Participation in sports and exercise is very important for the person with diabetes. One problem in controlling diabetes is weight gain. Weight gain occurs because insulin is a hormone that causes the body to store excess sugar as fat. In the teen years, gaining weight can be damaging to the student's self-image, and teenagers often permit their blood sugar to run high in order to lose weight. The key to keeping insulin needs down and staying slim and healthy is regular exercise. Thus participation in exercise and sports is vital for the well-being of affected students.

However, newly added or excessive exercise can lower blood sugar too much. Students must realize in scheduling their own exercise that the best time to engage in physical activities is after a meal. If the activity is done longer than two hours after a meal, the student may need a snack before the exercise or sport. Similarly, if the exercise is particularly strenuous and lasts more than 45 minutes, the student also will need extra carbohydrates.

A good supplement for exercise times is one of the commercially available sports drinks. These products not only supply extra sugar but also the extra minerals needed to replace those lost through perspiration. Fruit juice is a heavier carbohydrate source and may cause stomach cramping in some individuals. Usually, eight ounces of a sports drink every 45 to 60 minutes is sufficient to replace lost carbohydrates. However, the exercising student also may need to drink extra water to prevent dehydration from excessive perspiration.

If the student is doing regular strenuous exercise, such as running with the track team, it would be wise for him or her to monitor blood sugar levels before and after the exercise. Doing so not only gives information to prevent low blood sugar reactions but also helps the student know how much carbohydrate "loading" is needed to attain a specific blood sugar level during the exercise.

*Driver's Education.* In working with adolescents who have diabetes, parents and teachers may find that students' motivation to obtain a driver's license also is a good motivation to control their diabetes. In most states, an individual must be seizure-free for one year before being licensed to drive. After obtaining a driver's license, the student with diabetes should check his or her blood sugar as a safety precaution prior to driving, just like putting on a seat belt. Drivers with diabetes also should carry glucose tablets and peanut-butter crackers in the glovebox for emergencies, rather than rely on being able to stop for a convenient snack or soft drink. Wearing diabetes identification jewelry also is important. If the student is in an accident and becomes unconscious, emergency medical personnel will need to know that he or she has diabetes.

*Sex Education.* Many middle and high schools do a good job in health classes of informing adolescents about the health risks of early sexual activity and about pregnancy prevention. But not all adolescents heed the advice of their parents and teachers. Students with diabetes need to have specific information about sexual matters as they relate to diabetes. For example, young men may become impotent if their diabetes is poorly controlled. Young women with poorly controlled diabetes are at far greater risk of having a difficult pregnancy, a child with birth defects, or a still-born child than are their healthy peers. There is no reason why a young woman with IDDM cannot have healthy children; however, pregnancies should be carefully planned, and the individual's diabetes should be well-controlled for several months prior to the pregnancy.

Students with diabetes also should be aware that the likelihood of their offspring developing diabetes is only 4% to 6% greater than for the general population.

*Discipline.* Students with diabetes, like all students, occasionally need to be disciplined for infractions of school or classroom rules. However, such discipline should not involve eliminating an activity, such as recess or physical education, that can affect the student's control of diabetes. Teachers should use other appropriate methods of discipline.

Also, teachers should be aware that unusual acting out or sudden changes in behavior may indicate a low blood sugar reaction. In such cases, the student's blood sugar level should be tested. If no meter is available to test for low blood sugar, the teacher can not harm the student by treating the student for low blood sugar to see if the situation improves.

## Low Blood Sugar Reactions and Their Treatment

In September 1993 a landmark study, published in the *New England Journal of Medicine*, confirmed that effective diabetes control can help prevent long-term complications from the disease. In school settings, the involvement of several professionals in a health care team will ensure what health experts call "tight control." Tight control involves more than two injections of insulin a day or an insulin pump, frequent blood sugar monitoring, and frequent visits and consultations with the medical health care team. It involves developing and maintaining a lifestyle that keeps the individual's glucose level within the normal range. Overwhelmingly, evidence from this study demonstrated that keeping the blood sugar as close to normal as possible significantly reduces the risk of kidney disease, eye disease, and nerve disease. However, the study also revealed that tight control increased the risks of low blood sugar episodes three-fold.

For this reason, most health professionals do not recommend tight control for the child who has not yet reached puberty. In fact, the American Diabetes Association's goals for diabetes management in children is to promote normal growth and development while preventing severe high or low blood sugars. Preventing severe low blood sugar reactions is extremely important for the child under the age of seven. A severe low blood sugar reaction is characterized by the individual needing assistance in order to eat or drink, becoming unconscious, or having a seizure. If a student has frequent, severe low blood sugar episodes, the development of his or her brain can be affected and, as a result, the student may have a lower IQ than normally would be expected.

Severe low blood sugar readings often can be prevented by allowing the student to eat snacks and meals on time and through early detection of mildly low blood sugar. Mild low blood sugars are common. However, a student with diabetes, like anyone else, can become too preoccupied with activities to notice the early signs. When a young child, in particular, does experience a low blood sugar reaction and is treated, the teacher and the student should take time to reflect on the event and to talk about the way the child felt during the low blood sugar reaction. This discussion will help the young student learn how to recognize the signs.

Early signs of low blood sugar include: inability to concentrate, irritability, heart racing, headache, sudden perspiration, hunger, pallor, weakness, shakiness, nervousness, and numbness, especially around the mouth and tongue. Moderate to severe signs include: mental dullness, severe drowsiness, slurred speech, staggered walk, blurred or double vision, glassy eyes, such irrational behavior as combativeness or uncontrolled crying, confusion, and amnesia. Extremely severe signs are loss of consciousness or seizure. Teachers need to learn which early signs are likely for each student with diabetes in his or her classroom, and parents usually can provide this information.

*Treatment.* Treatment of low blood sugar involves feeding the child in order to quickly raise the blood sugar level. Staying calm is important, because overreacting will cause the student to feel embarrassed and different and may make the young child avoid telling the teacher about low blood sugar symptoms the next time.

Raising the blood sugar level quickly is important. Therefore, feeding the student a simple sugar is recommended as a quick treatment. Examples of simple sugar snacks are:

- a half cup of fruit juice;
- a half cup of nondiet soda;
- a small tube of cake-decorating gel or icing;
- 5 to 7 Lifesaver candies;
- 2 or 3 packets of sugar; or
- 5 sugar cubes.

Several commercial products also are available, such as glucose tablets and glucose gel in tubes. The glucose tablets are convenient for children to carry around in their bookbags or pockets. Unlike candy, they are not particularly tempting to eat; and they do not melt in the heat.

After treating the student with the simple sugar, experts recommend that the teacher wait 10 to 15 minutes before feeding the student anything else. If the student eats food with protein or fat right away, the action of the simple sugar will be slowed, and the child will not get over the low blood sugar episode as quickly. After the 10 or 15 minutes, if the child feels better, the student may eat 3 or 4 peanut-butter crackers or simply have lunch in order to prevent another low blood sugar episode. If the student does not feel better, then the simple sugar feeding should be repeated and another 10 or 15 minutes should be allowed to pass before the teacher allows the child eat normally. After the student has eaten and feels better, he or she should be able to resume normal activity.

Young children, in particular, should be praised for letting the teacher know about low blood sugar feelings. Such communication is a sign of maturity and shows that the youngster is moving toward self-management. If the young child does not recognize low blood sugar symptoms and the teacher notices a lack of coordination or a change in behavior or concentration, then after treating the child, it will be important for the teacher to discuss the episode with the child. In this way, the child will begin to learn how to self-manage the disease. Teachers do not need to telephone the parents when a mild low blood sugar episode occurs. But they should send a note home explaining the circumstances of the episode — such as during or after physical exercise — the time of day, how the episode was treated, and the student's response. This information helps parents adjust insulin dosage or meals to prevent additional episodes.

Adolescents tend to be more private than younger children about their diabetes management. Teachers in middle and high schools should encourage students with diabetes to keep a simple sugar — such as glucose tablets or a four-ounce juice box and a pack of peanut-butter or cheese crackers — in a bookbag or pocket. If the student feels the symptoms of low blood sugar during a class or other school activity, the simple sugar can be consumed without disturbing the class. If adolescents do not want to eat in front of their classmates, then they should be given permission to eat at their convenience, such as between classes, in the locker room, or while riding the school bus.

Teachers should not make a big fuss about eating snacks or treating low blood sugar. They can help students who are reluctant to self-manage because they are embarrassed by asking them to think about which would be more embarrassing, passing out in front of everyone or eating a small box of raisins. Health professionals also can work with the student to adjust insulin dosage in order to keep extra eating to a minimum.

*Severe low blood sugar reactions.* Severe low blood sugar reactions happen from time to time, even with the best precautions. Most parents of children with diabetes keep on hand an emergency injection, called glucagon, to treat severe low blood sugar episodes when the child cannot swallow or is having a seizure. It usually is not necessary for school personnel to keep glucagon on hand. If student passes out during a low blood sugar episode, a gel form of glucose, such as cake icing, can be squirted between the cheeks and gums and massaged in. The teacher or other school personnel then should call 911 or the local emergency number for help.

If the affected student has not passed out but is acting incoherent, the gel form of sugar again is the best treatment to use. It gets into the system faster and is easier to use than trying to pour juice or soda into the student's mouth. However, if juice or a nondiet soda is all that is available, then it should be used.

If a student has a seizure, the teacher should stay with the student, clear objects away from the student to prevent accidental injury, and call 911 or the local emergency number. Once the seizure subsides, the teacher can squirt the gel cake icing or glucose inside the student's cheeks and massage it in. The teacher should not attempt to put anything in the student's mouth *during* the seizure.

While a severe low blood sugar episode may occur at school, such episodes are more likely to happen during the night, for example, if the student skips a bedtime snack or the snack is inadequate. School personnel who supervise students on overnight field trips need to be aware of this information.

## High Blood Sugar Reactions

High blood sugar levels do not create acute reactions. However, management of high blood sugar also can affect the school day for the student. If the student experiences high blood sugar sufficient to produce ketones in his or her urine, the parents should notify the school so that teachers can encourage the student to drink more water than usual. This probably will mean that the teacher also will need to tolerate the student asking to use the restroom more often.

When ketones are present, the student should not participate in vigorous physical exercise or physical education classes. Ketones indicate that the body is under stress. If the student exercises during this time, thereby adding more stress, the blood sugar level often rises even further, thus worsening the situation.

A student's concentration during the school day also can be affected by high blood sugar. Students who fall asleep after eating lunch usually are experiencing post-meal high blood sugar. This reaction is common among teenagers who typically eat foods such as pizza and French fries for lunch. When such reactions affect a student's academic performance, they should be discussed with the student. Teachers then should contact the student's parents if no improvement is seen. If the student is eating a balanced lunch and still experiencing high blood sugar reactions, they may need to have their insulin dosage adjusted.

All students, but adolescents in particular, need to learn how to manage their diabetes independently. Teenagers often behave as though they are invulnerable. They take risks and experiment in all sorts of ways that parents and teachers attempt to discourage, often without success. When students with diabetes choose to smoke tobacco, consume alcohol, or use drugs, they greatly increase their risks for diabetes complications that are both acute and long term. One difference between teens with diabetes and others is that adolescents with diabetes may use their illness as a focus for risk-taking. Skipping insulin injections, skipping meals, or bingeing are not uncommon behaviors and usually will be discovered by the parent or the medical team. Fortunately, most youngsters learn to take fewer risks and move into successful self-management of their diabetes.

# Chapter Eight

# Epilepsy, or Seizure Disorders

Epilepsy is the general label for more than 20 types of seizure disorders. Characterized by repetitive seizures in an otherwise healthy individual, epilepsy occurs most often in childhood. In some cases, a child will outgrow the seizure disorder. But epilepsy also can start during the teen years. Seizures that occur from high fever, insulin shock in diabetes, or an illness that affects the brain are not classified as epilepsy.

Epileptic seizures are characterized by uncontrollable, excessive activity in all or part of the central nervous system (CNS). Epilepsy is symptomatic of some form of brain defect, and the type of seizure that occurs will depend on the area of the CNS that is affected.

The central nervous system, which is like the body's computer, comprises the brain, the spinal cord, and more than 100 billion nerves. The CNS controls both conscious and subconscious functions and is composed of three major levels. The first level of function occurs at the spinal cord and controls walking movements, reflexes that allow one to pull away from an object, reflexes that help one to stiffen the legs against gravity so that standing is possible, and reflexes that control some blood vessels and stomach and intestinal movements.

The second level, the lower brain, controls the subconscious activities of the body, such as salivation, emotions such as anger and excitement, reactions to pain or pleasure, and sexual activities.

At the third level is the higher brain, which controls memory and thought processes. The higher brain cannot function without the lower centers of the nervous system intact. The lower centers of the CNS can function to some degree without the higher level, but they are likely to be imprecise.

Each area of the CNS has a certain level of electrical excitability. In a person predisposed to epilepsy, the electrical activity in an area can rise above its normal threshold, which causes a seizure. In some instances, seizures are difficult to recognize. A person having a seizure may simply stare blankly for a few seconds, or a particular area of the person's body may twitch. Rapid, uncontrolled eye blinking can be a sign that the individual is having a seizure.

In other cases, the seizure is overt. The person who suffers a severe seizure may experience uncontrolled jerking accompanied by suspended breathing, which is known as a convulsion.

## Types of Seizures and How to Respond to Them

Most seizures fall into seven types: 1) the tonic-clonic, or grand mal, seizure; 2) the absence, or petit mal, seizure; 3) the simple partial seizure; 4) the partial complex, or temporal lobe, seizure; 5) the atonic seizure, or drop attack; 6) the myoclonic seizure; and 7) infantile spasms.

*Grand Mal Seizure.* When most people think of an epileptic seizure, they picture a grand mal seizure or convulsions. This type of seizure usually begins with a sudden cry followed immediately by unconsciousness. If the individual is standing or sitting, he or she will fall down or may fall out of a chair or desk when the seizure begins. Body rigidity is closely followed by generalized muscle jerking and clenched teeth. Breathing can be suspended temporarily, and the skin and lips can take on a bluish color. The individual also may lose bowel or bladder control.

A grand mal seizure usually lasts no more than two or three minutes before normal breathing resumes. For a short time following the seizure, the individual will appear to be deeply asleep. When the individual begins to recover consciousness, confusion

74

and fatigue are the first signs. These sensations are followed by a full recovery to consciousness. The entire seizure and recovery period usually takes 10 to 20 minutes.

Occasionally the student with epilepsy may experience a warning that a seizure is impending. This warning can range from a odd taste in the mouth or the perception of an odd smell to seeing flashing lights. If the student is in tune to these signals, he or she may lie down on the floor to prevent injury from falling. However, in most cases, seizures commence without warning.

If he or she has not already fallen, when a student begins to convulse the teachers should assist the student to lie down on the floor. The teacher or other students should move nearby objects, such as desks and chairs, away from the affected student. The teacher may place a folded jacket or a soft object under the student's head to protect against injury and should loosen any tight clothing from around the student's neck. The teacher should not put anything in the student's mouth or try to hold or restrain the student in any way.

The teacher should stay with the affected student during the seizure and should reassure other students in the room that the student will be all right after the seizure has passed. In some cases, other students can be helpful, for example, by timing a seizure in order to document the episode for the affected student's health care provider. When the affected student's jerking motion stops, the teacher can turn the student on his or her side and speak reassuringly as consciousness returns. The student should be allowed to keep an extra change of clothing at school in case it is needed. If the student bit his or her tongue during the seizure, he or she should be allowed to rinse the mouth with salt water.

Convulsions can call for emergency action. A student who is experiencing a grand mal seizure should never be given cardiopulmonary resuscitation (CPR) during the convulsion. However, CPR is appropriate if the student is not breathing after he or she stops jerking. Emergency personnel should be summoned whenever CPR is used, if the convulsive jerking lasts longer than five minutes, if multiple seizures occur, and if the affected student is pregnant, has diabetes, or is injured during the seizure.

*Petit Mal Seizure.* Absence, or petit mal, seizures are the most difficult to recognize, but they are the most common type of seizure in children. A petit mal seizure produces a momentary loss of awareness that may last only a few seconds. Therefore, such a seizure can be mistaken for lack of attention, deliberately ignoring adult instructions, or daydreaming. What differentiates the absence seizure from these other behaviors is that it can interrupt an ongoing activity. Absence seizures also may be accompanied by facial movements, such as chewing or lip smacking, rapid blinking, or subtle arm movements. The affected student is totally unaware of what is going on during the seizure and quickly returns to full awareness of his or her surroundings once the seizure has stopped.

When such a seizure is first noticed, the student should be referred for medical evaluation. Failure to recognize and treat such seizures may lead to learning difficulties simply because the affected student may miss key points of lessons. Teachers need to be aware of students who suffer petit mal seizures and ensure that such students understand important aspects of lessons they may have missed. Rarely is any type of aid needed for the student during the seizure itself.

*Simple Partial Seizure.* Simple partial seizures are limited to one area in the brain, and the affected student will not lose consciousness. Such seizures may be manifested by jerking that can begin in one area of the body and travel to another area. The student will have no control over these movements. In some cases, this type of seizure can spread through the body and become a convulsive seizure.

When the affected student experiences a distorted environment, the disorder is termed a partial *sensory* seizure. During this type of seizure, the student may see, hear, or smell things that are not present and may experience unexplained fear, sadness, anger, or joy. These sensations may be accompanied by nausea. The student may recall the experience of the seizure as frightening, and so the teacher should provide reassurance during and after the episode.

Partial seizures are not easy for teachers to recognize. Often they initially are labeled as acting out, bizarre behavior, hysteria, mental illness, psychosomatic illness, parapsychological, or a mystical experience. When a partial seizure is recognized, the teacher seldom will need to provide specific aid unless a convulsive seizure follows the partial seizure. If convulsions should occur, the teacher should protect the student from injury in the same manner described for the grand mal seizure.

*Complex Partial Seizure.* A complex partial seizure can be mistaken for intoxication from alcohol or drugs, sleepwalking, mental illness, or just disorderly conduct. It usually begins with a blank stare, then a chewing motion followed by some kind of a random motion, such as picking at the clothes. The affected student will be unaware of his or her surroundings, may seem dazed, and may mumble. His or her actions will seem clumsy, and the student may try to pick up objects or take off clothes. Fear also is a common reaction, and the student may try to run or leave the room. If the teacher or other students attempt to restrain the affected student, the student may resist by struggling or flailing.

Students who are affected by complex partial seizures usually develop a pattern of actions during the seizure, and that pattern will be followed in each seizure. Such seizures seldom last more than one or two minutes, but the student may feel confused afterward. The teacher should speak calmly and reassuringly to the student having the seizure as well as to the other students in the classroom. The teacher can gently guide the affected student away from hazards, such as machinery or laboratory equipment; but the teacher should not grab hold of the student unless there is an immediate danger, such as the student walking in front of a moving vehicle or falling down stairs.

The teacher should not expect the affected student to obey verbal instructions during the seizure or shortly afterward. Therefore, the teacher should stay with the student until the student regains complete awareness of his or her surroundings. The student probably will not remember any part of the seizure.

*Atonic Seizure or Drop Attack.* This type of seizure also may be called *akinetic*. The affected student will suddenly become unconscious and fall to the floor. The student will not experience muscle contractions or jerking. After 10 to 60 seconds, the student will be able to stand and walk again. This type of seizure often is associated with some degree of mental illness. However, atonic seizures in an otherwise healthy individual can be mistaken for clumsiness, drunkenness, or an acute illness.

If this type of seizure is likely, the student may need to wear a helmet to prevent head injuries. No specific physical aid is indicated for the affected student unless he or she is injured by the fall. However, the teacher should always provide emotional support and reassurance.

*Myoclonic Seizures.* These seizures produce sudden, brief, and massive muscle jerks that can involve part or all of the body. The affected student may drop what he or she is holding or fall out of a chair without any warning. Thus a myoclonic seizure can easily be mistaken for clumsiness or poor coordination. The student who suffers a myoclonic seizure usually does not lose consciousness.

The teacher does not need to provide any specific care during the seizure. However, follow-up first aid may be needed if the student is injured during the seizure.

*Infantile Spasm.* Infantile spasms usually occur in young children between the ages of three months and two years. Therefore, early childhood teachers and childcare providers need to understand that this type of spasm is characterized by clusters of sudden, quick movements. Such spasms can be hard to detect in infants, because babies often jerk their limbs. The key to recognizing infantile spasms is discerning patterns of jerking movements. If a child is sitting up, his or her head typically will fall forward and the arms will jerk forward during the spasm. If the seizure occurs while the child is lying down, his or her knees will be drawn up and the arms and head will flex and jerk forward as if the child is reaching out for support.

Teachers who observe suspected infantile spasms should discuss their observations with the child's parents. Generally, no intervention will be necessary during a spasm.

## Emergency Circumstances

In summary, most seizures do not require specific emergency management and usually are resolved without any residual problems for the affected student. However, as we have noted in several of the preceding descriptions, occasionally emergencies can arise. Teachers should contact emergency personnel in the following circumstances:

- if a serious injury occurs during a seizure;
- if a student experiences a seizure for the first time;
- if the student who experiences a seizure has diabetes or is pregnant;
- if a second seizure begins before the student regains consciousness from the first seizure;
- if the seizure continues for longer than five minutes;
- if the seizure occurs while the student is swimming or there is a possibility that the student has ingested water;
- if the student still experiences difficulty in walking 20 minutes after the seizure has ended; and
- if the student vomits, complains of a persistent headache, has difficulty seeing, or has dilated pupils or pupils of unequal size.

## Routine Management for Students with Epilepsy

Teachers should deal with seizures in a manner similar to how they are dealt with in the student's home. Parents and teachers should avoid becoming overly protective. Students with epilepsy need age-appropriate responsibilities for managing their own illness.

An initial meeting that includes affected parents, teachers, school bus drivers, coaches, and other appropriate personnel should discuss the student's medical condition and plan how to handle seizures that occur during classes or school events. Parents should provide written medical information for the student's file that includes details about the type and frequency of seizures, medications and their side effects, and any performance or activity limitations that may be specified by the student's physician. Children with epilepsy occasionally will need to be excused from school for medical appointments and should not be penalized for such absences.

More than 50% of all people with epilepsy can completely control their seizures with medication. Another 30% can use various medicines to improve the management of their illness, such as decreasing the number or severity of seizures. For example, medicine may be used to reduce grand mal seizures to petit mal seizures. However, a small percentage of individuals with epilepsy cannot be helped by medication. For some of these individuals, recent advances in surgery may be helpful.

Many medicines for epilepsy produce side effects. Therefore, it is helpful for teachers to know some of the common medicines and some of the potential side effects that affected students may experience in the classroom. The most common medicines used to control epilepsy in young people are phenobarbital, phenytoin (Dilantin), ethosuximide (Zarontin), valproate (Depakane or Depakote), and carbamazepine (Tegretol). Common side effects of these medicines include drowsiness, hyperactivity, decreased coordination, double vision, confusion, slurred speech, tremors, nausea, increased body hair, sleep disturbances, loss of appetite, stomach aches, and gum swelling. Usually these side effects are minimal and do not disrupt the school day for the student. But it is important for teachers and other school personnel to be observant and report any side effects that students with seizure disorders experience. These observations can be an important part of effective medical management for the affected students.

Some specific areas of concern are exercise and physical education, driving, academic performance, and behavior.

*Exercise and Physical Education.* Exercise is important for the proper growth and development of all children. Students with epilepsy may need to be restricted from certain physical exercises but, in general, do not need to be stringently limited. Students with well-controlled epilepsy may need no limits on physical activity. Other students may need to be restricted from certain activities, such as playing on monkey bars or swinging. Special care or restrictions may be needed with regard to water activities and swimming. Parent and physician information should be carefully reviewed.

*Driving.* Older students who wish to participate in driver's training can be allowed to do so. However, some students may be restricted from behind-the-wheel training if their seizures are poorly controlled. Most states require the student with a seizure disorder to file a medical statement prior to being issued a driver's license.

*Academic Performance.* Most students with epilepsy have average IQ's and are able to keep up with regular classroom work. If a student achieves lower scores than expected, teachers may want to consider possible side effects from antiseizure medications in determining a cause. Teachers should inform parents if their child seems to be excessively sleepy or lacks energy during the school day, as it may be necessary to adjust the student's medication. Sometimes, unrecognized seizure activity in the brain also may be interfering with thought processes.

*Behavior.* The average student with a seizure disorder will not exhibit unusual behavior problems and will respond to discipline as any other student might respond. If behavior problems do arise, teachers should consider a variety of sources, such as the possibility of an additional underlying brain problem, side effects from medicine, the student's feelings of anxiety or low self-esteem, and overprotection or overindulgence by the student's parents. Identifying the source of the behavior problem will be the teacher's first step in finding a solution, but this may be a difficult task. The teacher should enlist the help of the parents, the student's physician, and any other health and education professionals. In most cases, the student should be included in the discussion.

## Helping Classmates Understand

When a seizure occurs in school, the entire classroom is affected. Seizures can look very frightening. Unless handled appropriately, particularly in the early grades, the fear generated by witnessing the seizure can lead to other students being afraid of the youngster who had the seizure. This may then lead to teasing and ridicule. However, the teacher can take steps to prepare students so that the occurrence of a seizure will cause only minimal disruption.

In many cases, teachers can minimize these negative aspects by teaching their classes about seizures in advance of an occurrence, but in so doing they need to be aware of the parents' and the student's rights and desires for privacy. The school nurse can be a good resource of information for teaching about seizure disorders.

After a student experiences a seizure, other students who have witnessed the seizure may have fears or questions. These should be addressed immediately. The student who experienced the seizure also may be included in this discussion. Or that student may choose not to participate but should be told later about the discussion.

All students, but younger children in particular, need appropriate, factual information. They need reassurance that what happened poses no danger to them or to the student having the seizure. Some key points include:

- defining the occurrence as a seizure;
- explaining that a seizure occurs when the brain sends mixed signals to the body, that a seizure last only a short time, and that the body recovers quickly after a seizure;
- noting that seizures and epilepsy are not diseases and cannot be "caught" by others who come into contact with the affected student; and
- explaining that the best thing other students can do for the student who experiences a seizure is to keep him or her safe during the occurrence — and then be a good friend afterward.

A caring, well-informed teacher can help prevent the damaging social impact that epilepsy and other seizure disorders can have for an affected student.

# Chapter Nine

# Sickle Cell Disease

Sickle cell disease is a term that describes several inherited blood disorders caused by the abundance of sickle hemoglobin (Hb S) in the blood. Hemoglobin is a protein in the blood that carries oxygen from the lungs to all parts of the body and causes the blood cells to be red in color. In the United States, sickle cell disease is most common among African Americans; however, it also frequently occurs among people of Arabian, Caribbean, Iranian, Indian, Latin American, and Mediterranean ancestry. About 1 in 400 African Americans is born with sickle cell disease.

In people with normal hemoglobin (Hb A), the red blood cells are doughnut shaped and flexible in order to flow easily through the many tiny capillaries in the body. When red blood cells are mostly sickle hemoglobin, they still can transport oxygen efficiently, but these cells change shape when their oxygen is released to the tissues. The cells take on a sickle or crescent shape until they receive more oxygen from the lungs and return to their original disk shape.

Over time, the cells with Hb S become damaged and remain in a rigid sickle shape. These damaged cells are unable to travel easily through the capillaries and often cluster together, causing blockages in the blood vessels. When the vessels are blocked or partially blocked, the red blood cells may not able to supply some parts of the body with enough oxygen. Consequently, organ damage can occur.

At birth, a baby with sickle cell disease looks and acts normal; but after about three to six months, he or she may be unusually tired and cranky, have a poor appetite, and have pale lips, tongue, and palms. Although sickle cell disease is inherited, both parents usually are healthy because they have sickle cell trait, not sickle cell disease. Persons with the sickle cell trait have both Hb A and Hb S in their red blood cells, but the dominant hemoglobin is Hb A. For example, about 10% of African Americans have the sickle cell trait but do not develop sickle cell disease.

When both parents have the sickle cell trait, there is a 25% chance that the child will develop sickle cell disease. The chance of developing sickle cell disease is 50% if one parent has the sickle cell trait and the other parent has sickle cell disease. If both parents have sickle cell disease, their children invariably develop the disease.

## Medical Conditions Related to Sickle Cell Disease

*Sickle Cell Anemia and Its Management.* Anemia is a condition that occurs when the number of red blood cells in the body fall below normal. Many individuals with sickle cell disease suffer from anemia because the disease process causes early destruction of cells. Normal red blood cells with Hb A live about 120 days, but the sickle cells with Hb S survive only 12 days. Because the body is unable to produce red blood cells quickly enough to replace the short-lived sickle cells, the person develops anemia.

Although students with sickle cell anemia can run, jump, play, swim, bike, and participate in other physical activities, they must be careful not to overexert themselves. While these students certainly are not invalids, they do have some physical limitations. In most cases, young people with sickle cell anemia know their tolerance level and can be trusted to make correct decisions. When questions arise, the teacher should talk to the student or contact the parent or guardian.

Teachers should fully involve students with sickle cell anemia in all class activities. However, they must recognize that affected students may need more rest time (or recovery time) than other students after physical activities. In many cases, affected students who are unable to actively participate in physical games may be involved as coaching assistants or referees.

One concern when a student has sickle cell anemia is the risk of suddenly worsened anemia, or an aplastic crisis. Although a rare complication of sickle cell disease, an aplastic crisis often is associated with a viral infection that causes the body to temporarily cease producing red blood cells. Another rare complication of sickle cell anemia is acute splenic sequestration. This condition occurs mostly in preschoolers when the spleen captures the sickle cells, thereby causing acute anemia. If a student appears to be paler than usual or the symptoms of anemia suddenly worsen, the teacher must inform the student's parent in order to provide prompt medical attention.

*Painful Episodes.* Having a painful episode, or sickle cell crisis, is the most common recurring condition associated with sickle cell disease. The crisis is caused when the sickle cells accumulate and adhere together in the blood stream. As the mass of sickle cells increases in size, the blood vessels become clogged, making it difficult or impossible for the blood to circulate. The reduced blood flow deprives tissues of oxygen and is accompanied by pain in the affected area of the body. Typically, such pain is centered in the chest, abdomen, arms, and legs; but it can occur in other parts of the body.

People with sickle cell disease often describe a painful episode as excruciating, tormenting pain that comes on gradually. The frequency and severity of pain associated with painful episodes vary greatly among individuals with sickle cell disease. Although the average painful episode lasts from four to six days, a sickle cell crisis may include several cycles of increasing and decreasing pain over a period of time from several hours to several weeks. In a few instances, people with sickle cell disease state that they are in constant pain.

In many cases, a mild painful episode can be treated at home or school with oral medicines, such as aspirin or acetaminophen (for example, Tylenol). Some individuals also require an oral narcotic, such as codeine, to reduce the pain.

If the sickle cell crisis is moderate or severe, injections of stronger narcotics, such as meperidine (Demerol) or morphine may be required. Occasionally, when being treated for pain, students with sickle cell disease are not given adequate medicine because caregivers fear that the medication will create a drug dependency. Although drug addiction is extremely rare in students with sickle cell disease, teachers should alert parents or the student's health care team if students seem to be unusually dependent on drugs.

In addition to controlling the pain of sickle cell disease with medication, painful episodes are managed with fluid intake and by eliminating precipitating events. Dehydration tends to promote sickle cell adhesion; therefore, drinking increased fluids is a foundation for controlling painful episodes. However, sickle cell disease also may damage the kidneys so that they are unable to retain adequate water. Consequently, the kidneys can release too much fluid, thereby increasing the risk of a painful episode. Guidelines from the National Institute of Health suggest that adults with sickle cell disease drink three to five liters of fluid each day and that children drink approximately one-tenth liter per kilogram of body weight each day.

If a student is having a painful episode at school, the teacher should encourage the student to drink fluids, such as water, ice tea, and soft drinks. Fluids also should be encouraged when the student is not experiencing a sickle cell crisis, especially during conditions that could precipitate a painful episode. Such conditions include increased physical activity, warm air temperatures, exposure to extreme cold, and any other activity that might constrict the blood vessels, cause the body to lose fluids, or increase the body's need for oxygen. In addition to drinking fluids, students with sickle cell disease can minimize the likelihood of a painful episode by maintaining good general health through proper diet, sufficient rest, and attention to personal hygiene.

When a painful episode occurs, the cause also may be an underlying illness. These illnesses are often infections or other medical conditions that must be identified and treated. Other causes of painful episodes cited by people with sickle cell disease are anxiety, depression, and exhaustion. Sometimes, two or more interrelated problems precipitate the sickle cell crisis. For example, a student with a cold may experience stress and fatigue from trying to keep up with the class. When the student has sickle cell disease, the effects of that tension and the underlying illness may produce a painful episode. Although many precipitating events can be identified, often the painful crisis just happens and a cause cannot be determined.

An affected student's parents or physician should provide the school with information about how the student should manage a mild painful episode while at school. However, students should be taken to a physician immediately if they experience severe abdominal pain, extremity weakness or loss of function, acute joint swelling, fever above 101°F (38°C), lethargy, dehydration, pallor, or pain not relieved by conservative measures.

*Other Medical Concerns.* The leading cause of death in young children with sickle cell disease is infection. The most common indication of infection is fever, and any fever should be evaluated promptly. If a student with sickle cell disease has a fever at school, school personnel must inform the parents so that they can provide adequate medical attention. Mild infections may be treated at home with oral medicines, or the student may have to be admitted to a hospital for intravenous antibiotics. Educators should be prepared to contact the student's health care provider directly if the parent or guardian cannot be reached.

If a fever is accompanied by a cough and an increased respiratory rate, the student may have pneumonia. Students with sickle cell disease are 100 times more likely to contract pneumonia than students in the general population. When the symptoms of pneumonia are present, school personnel must immediately contact the parents or the student's medical provider so that the student can be diagnosed and receive treatment.

Another medical complication that affects students with sickle cell disease is gallstones. As the disease causes the early destruction of red blood cells, large amounts of hemoglobin are released. The hemoglobin molecules further break down into bilirubin and contribute to the formation of gallstones. Gallstones may produce such problems as nausea, vomiting, right upper abdominal pain, and shoulder pain. Often the increased levels of bilirubin will cause the white part of the affected student's eyes to take on a yellowish tint. When any of these symptoms occur at school, the teacher should make the student as comfortable as possible and alert the parents. Gallstones can be serious, and gallbladder surgery may be required. When surgery is needed, the student probably will miss one to two weeks of school. The teacher should provide assignments that the student can work on at home while recovering from the operation. If the recovery period is extended, the school should arrange homebound instruction or special tutoring.

When sickle cell disease causes localized circulatory problems that deprive body tissues of oxygen and produce painful episodes, the disease can cause related problems. For example, when the hip lacks adequate blood flow, some of the bone dies, also causing severe pain. This condition, known as aseptic necrosis of the hip, limits the motion of the hip joint and can be disabling. Often, a brace is required to prevent the hip from dislocating and to relieve the pain. Therefore, teachers should be alert to any change of gait or pain in the hip joint experienced by the student with sickle cell disease. If a student must wear a brace, the teacher should be sensitive to the social and psychological effects of being "different" and work to minimize those effects by rearranging the classroom or seating arrangement in order to provide the student with unrestricted access.

An infrequent but damaging complication of sickle cell disease is a stroke. Strokes occur in 6% to 12% of young people with sickle cell anemia. A stroke results when the blood vessels to areas of the brain are blocked by sickle cells and the resulting oxygen shortage causes brain tissue damage. Although some individuals completely recover from a stroke, frequently the consequences of a stroke are mental impairment or physical disability. If a stroke does occur, the student must receive periodic transfusions of packed red blood cells to reduce the risk of further impairment from another stroke. This treatment usually lasts for three or more years and eventually requires medication to remove excess iron that accumulates in the body because of the transfusions.

Visual signs of a stroke include headaches, paralysis, unusual weakness, imbalance, seizures, learning difficulty, difficulty with speech or vision, and changes in school performance. When a teacher observes stroke symptoms, he or she must call for emergency medical treatment.

## Psychological Issues

The physical manifestations of sickle cell disease may negatively affect the social and psychological well-being of the student. One example is the delayed growth and sexual maturity associated with sickle cell disease. The affected student may appear to be several years younger than his or her age peers. The onset of puberty in students with sickle cell disease is delayed, on average, about two years. During adolescence, the physically immature teenager may be embarrassed by his or her appearance. It is especially important for teachers to treat affected students according to their real age, not according to their younger appearance, and to give such students opportunities to use and display talents that do not depend on physical maturity.

Possibly the greatest obstacle to school success for students with sickle cell disease is having to be absent from school for medical reasons. Such absences often result in low academic achievement and the emotional stress that comes from trying to make up missed school work. In some cases, students with sickle cell disease miss more than 50 days during the school year. However, by planning carefully in advance of extended absences and by accommodating frequent sporadic absences, teachers can help affected students achieve success by effectively using the school time they have.

# Chapter Ten

# Other School Services

Teachers and other educators work with young people more often and for a longer time than anyone else outside the home. Indeed, an elementary classroom teacher may spend more time actively communicating with many children than the children's parents can spend during the few hours at home before and after school when their children are awake. As a result, teachers often are the first to notice physical, behavioral, or emotional changes in their students. Such changes may indicate that some form of intervention is needed.

For students who have a chronic illness, the intervention might be medical, educational, social, or psychological, or a combination of all of these. Most teachers understand the academic and social requirements of students, but few teachers know much about how to address the health needs of students, especially students with a chronic illness. Although teachers are not medical professionals, they should have the basic training, knowledge, and skills necessary to recognize the health care needs of their students and to intervene when necessary. Teachers also should know what to do in a medical emergency and how to refer the student to any required special services.

## Health-Related Resources for Educator Training

The primary community resource for health-related adult instruction in the United States is the American Red Cross. The Red Cross can provide more than 20 different types of health and safety courses. A good choice for educators is a basic course in cardiopulmonary resuscitation (CPR), leading to a CPR competency certificate. This course teaches participants how to deal with an emergency and how to prevent childhood injuries. In addition, the course teaches lifesaving skills that are necessary to help adults, children, and infants in health crisis situations.

Teachers who earn a CPR certificate may be able to provide a safer environment for all their students, not just those with a chronic illness. After completing the basic CPR course, educators may enroll in other courses and become qualified in different areas of first aid or in a higher level of CPR. The Red Cross also offers a course for children, titled Basic Aid Training, which is designed to teach younger students basic first aid.

Courses or seminars that present health information about chronic illnesses also are offered by medical associations and medical centers. For example, the American Diabetes Association maintains a speakers bureau whose members will present talks and seminars for school groups. Many local affiliates of the Epilepsy Foundation of America also offer a variety of training programs to help teachers and students better understand the disorder. Additionally, in many communities the local hospital, medical center, or health department often can provide one of their medical personnel to deliver a program. Advanced practice nurses, such as clinical nurse specialists or public health nurses, are knowledgeable about students with chronic illnesses and how educators can provide a more healthful classroom environment for them.

Teachers who know that there will be students with particular chronic illnesses in their classes can order a variety of training materials to help them understand the illnesses and how to help the students manage their disorders. The Arthritis Foundation, for example, publishes a pamphlet specifically for teachers who will be working with students who have arthritis. The Epilepsy Foundation, the American Diabetes Association, the National Cancer Institute, the Cystic Fibrosis Center, and the Duke University Comprehensive Sickle Cell Center are among the other organizations that provide similar materials.

In addition to written guides, many of these and other organizations offer videotapes for teachers and other school personnel. The Epilepsy Foundation, for example, can provide two 14-minute videotapes titled, *Seizure Disorders and the School*. Each tape shows real seizures in school-age children and information about seizure management. After viewing the tapes, many teachers feel more confident about working with students who have some form of epilepsy, because they better understand what to expect and know how to handle crisis situations. These and other resources can be ordered through the organizations listed in the Resources section.

Seminars, booklets, videotapes, and other training may not anticipate every question or concern of educators who are involved with chronically ill students. For answers to questions that arise, educators may be able to contact some organizations using a hotline telephone number. Members of the National Cancer Institute, for example, sponsor a toll-free Cancer Information Service to answer questions and listen to concerns. The service is available seven days a week at 1-800-422-6237. The information also can be provided in Spanish. Other hotlines can be found in the Resources section.

## Accessing Community Services

Teachers can provide a great deal of health-related information to students. They can help educate students about their illness, and they can help other students understand the circumstances of their peers who have a chronic illness. Sometimes, however, the need for specific education or assistance goes beyond the teacher's capacity to help. In those instances, teachers need to be familiar with community services that can provide the necessary assistance to students and their parents.

In some cases, students with a chronic illness do not have adequate support from family members. Lack of family support may range from minimal to severe, and each student's situation is unique. In most cases, the parent or guardian is the person primarily responsible for monitoring how well the young person controls the disease. The teacher supports the parent's efforts, but it is not the teacher's role to assume the function of the parent. If the student consistently experiences medical problems at school because of poor management of the illness, the teacher should advise the parent of the problem. It is then the parents' responsibility to intervene. On those occasions when the parents are not able to effectively handle the situation, a teacher or other school official may request a special service.

The purpose of the various special services is to provide what is needed to benefit the student and his or her family. Such special services can be many and varied. One special service can provide training to the student and family about how to better control the chronic illness. For example, a student with arthritis may be missing school because of stiffness and pain in the joints. The health care team may evaluate the situation and determine that the student's family is following the required regimen to control the disease but that the student is not performing the exercises properly. In this instance, the student and his or her family require additional training in correctly performing the special exercises. The health care team will refer the student and the parents to a physical therapist who will instruct the parents and student and then determine if the student properly accomplishes the exercises. After the intervention, the student will be evaluated for improved joint mobility and function and better school attendance.

A similar situation can occur with students who have diabetes. A teacher may notice that a student with diabetes often experiences symptoms of low blood glucose, such as feeling nervous and anxious. The teacher notifies the parent, but the symptoms of low blood glucose continue. When the student's health care team meets to discuss the problem, they discover that the student tests the glucose level regularly, takes insulin at the prescribed times, and even eats extra food before strenuous exercise. The team recommends that the student consult his or her doctor or diabetes educator to determine why the glucose level often is low. After an evaluation, the diabetes educator changes the student's insulin dose and meal plan and asks the student to record glucose levels at regular intervals. The teacher notices fewer symptoms of low glucose level and increased learning ability.

A severe lack of home support occurs when a family, for various reasons, is unable to cope with their child having a chronic illness. It usually becomes obvious to the teacher when the student is not receiving proper care. The student may be frequently absent from school, unable to function properly when in class, unable to control the disease, and often in need of emergency medical care. In such cases, the health care team will recommend special services, such as family counseling, intervention by a social worker, or visits by a home health care nurse. The severity of a case may result in the student being placed in foster care. Regardless of the situation, the goal of the health care team should be to provide an environment wherein the student is able to control his or her illness and receive an appropriate education.

## The School Health Advisory Council

As a result of the Education for Handicapped Children Act (Public Law 94-142), more recently recast as the Individuals with Disabilities Education Act (P.L. 101-476), schools are educating a greater number of students who have complex health needs that require case management and clinical services.

Historically, a school nurse provided health services to students; but this role has changed in recent years, in part because an increasing student-nurse ratio has limited the school's capacity for meeting student health needs. Although the American Nursing Association advises a student-nurse ratio of one nurse for 750 students, many schools and districts provide only one nurse for more than 1,000 students. Thus, in order to provide better school health care services, many schools and districts have formed school health advisory councils.

Health advisory councils address a variety of issues, such as school health services, health education, control of the school health environment, and compliance with federal and state laws regarding student health matters. A health advisory council should include health care providers, teachers, parents, administrators, and others who have a special interest in the health needs of all students. In most cases, if there is a single health advisory council for the district, each school should be represented by at least one staff member.

Recently, some school districts have developed comprehensive health programs that coordinate school and community services. Their activities usually are school-based and emphasize health education, a healthful school environment, physical education, health counseling, and healthy eating. In a few places, in-school health clinics are being established.

The North Carolina Center for Nursing provides an example of the mission, philosophy, and goals of a successful school health care program. Their mission and philosophy state that:

> the program is the school's contribution to the understanding, maintenance, and improvement of the health of pupils and school personnel through health services, health education, and healthful school living. While it is recognized that parents have the basic responsibility for the health of their children, the school has a legal and moral obligation to deal with existing health threats or problems. An alert, sensitive faculty and staff can impart to children knowledge, attitudes, and skills that will enhance the quality and continuity of their lives.

Based on this mission and philosophy, the goals of the health program are: 1) to prepare students to achieve their full potential through becoming responsible for their health decisions and practices, 2) to provide a healthy control on the environment, 3) to prevent and control communicable diseases, and 4) to identify and correct health problems that are a deterrent to learning.

Students with a chronic illness will benefit when schools have a mission, philosophy, and goals toward health care similar to these. It is vitally important for students to become responsible for their own health decisions — and to make good decisions.

The decisions that individuals with a chronic illnesses make concerning their disease when they are young have a profound effect on the quality of health they will experience throughout their lifetime. Many students, especially teenagers, act as though they are immortal. Thus they neglect their illness and lose control. By helping young people to understand the importance of making good health decisions, students with a chronic illness may be more likely to follow their medical regimens and reach their full potential.

Identifying and correcting health problems, the fourth goal above, also is vital to the maintenance of good student health and effective management of chronic illnesses. Just as teachers understand that they must be well trained to teach their subjects, many teachers now are recognizing that they also must be prepared to meet the health needs of their students. Administrators are supporting their teachers in this effort by accepting for renewal such credit courses as seminars on chronic illnesses and American Red Cross CPR and other training. By using the information from these courses, health-related publications, medical personnel, parents, students, and others, teachers will be better able to understand chronic illnesses, to recognize symptoms that need attention, to work effectively with parents and medical personnel to help students keep their disease in control, and to intervene when necessary to provide special services or to respond to an emergency.

Finally, perhaps one of the most important reasons that educators should be well informed is that a teacher can lessen the damaging social impact of a chronic illness on a student and thus help each student maximize his or her personal and academic potential.

# Resources

Below is a list of organizations that will provide teachers with more information about the chronic illnesses included in the previous chapters. In addition, the list includes sources of information for chronic illnesses not addressed in this book. Some of the listed organizations, such as the Clearinghouse on Disability Information, are able to provide information about a variety of medical conditions. Toll-free phone numbers are listed if they are available.

Readers with access to the World Wide Web will find the home page for the Centers for Disease Control and Prevention at http://www.cdc.gov/cdc.html.

In most communities, more information about chronic illness is available at the local health department. If there is not a local health department, the nearest major medical center or each state's Department of Health is an excellent resource. For a more comprehensive list of resources, consult the *Encyclopedia of Associations*, Section 8: Health and Medical Organizations, published by Gale Research Incorporated, International Thomson Publishing Company, New York. This reference work is updated annually and is available at most libraries, on CD-ROM, and on such popular online services as DIALOG or NEXIS.

Agency for Health Care Policy and Research
Publications Clearinghouse
P.O. Box 8547
Silver Springs, MD 20907
1-800-358-9295

American Cancer Society
1599 Clifton Road, NE
Atlanta, GA 30329
1-800-227-2345

American Diabetes Association
Diabetes Information Service Center
1660 Duke Street
Alexandria, VA 22314
1-800-232-3472

American Heart Association
7320 Greenville Avenue
Dallas, TX 75231
1-800-242-1793

American Lung Association
1740 Broadway
New York, NY 10019

American Medical Association
535 North Dearborn Street
Chicago, IL 60610

Arizona Consortium for Children with Chronic Illness
P.O. Box 2128
Phoenix, AZ 85001

Arthritis Foundation
P.O. Box 19000
Atlanta, GA 30326
1-800-283-7800

Association for the Care of Children's Health
3615 Wisconsin Ave., NW
Washington, DC 20016

Asthma and Allergy Foundation of America
1125 Fifteenth Street, NW, Suite 502
Washington, DC 20005
1-800-727-8462

CDC National Aids Clearinghouse
P.O. Box 6003
Rockville, MD 20849
1-800-458-5231

Chronic Illness Teaching Program
Department of Pediatrics and Human Development
B-240, Life Sciences Building
Michigan State University
East Lansing, MI 48824

Clearinghouse on Disability Information
Office of Special Education and Rehabilitative Services
Department of Education Room
3106 Switzer Building
230 C Street, SW
Washington, DC 20202

Coordination of Care for Chronically Ill Children Program
New York State Department of Health
Tower Building, Room 878
Empire State Plaza
Albany, NY 12237

Cystic Fibrosis Foundation
6931 Arlington Road
Bethesda, MD 20814
1-800-344-4823

Duke University Comprehensive Sickle Cell Center
Box 3934
Duke University Medical Center
Durham, NC 27710

Epilepsy Foundation of America
4351 Garden City Drive
Landover, MD 20785
1-800-332-1000

Juvenile Diabetes Foundation
23 East 26th Street
New York, NY 10010
1-800-533-2873

Muscular Dystrophy Association
3300 E. Sunrise Drive
Tucson, AZ 85718

National Association for Sickle Cell Disease, Inc.
4221 Wilshire Boulevard, Suite 360
Los Angeles, CA 90010
1-800-421-8453

National Cancer Institute
9000 Rockville Pike
Bethesda, MD 20892
1-800-422-6237

National Multiple Sclerosis Society
208 East 42nd Street
New York, NY 10017
1-800-344-4867

Parent Advocacy Coalition for Educational Rights
4826 Chicago Avenue, South
Minneapolis, MN 55417

U.S. Public Health Service
5600 Fishers Lane
Rockville, MD 20857